Just a Click Away

Just a Click Away
Advertising on the Internet

Barbara K. Kaye
Valdosta State University

Norman J. Medoff
Northern Arizona University

Allyn and Bacon
Boston • London • Toronto • Sydney • Tokyo • Singapore

Series Editor: Karon Bowers
Editorial Assistant: Jennifer Becker
Marketing Manager: Jacqueline Aaron
Production Editor: Christopher H. Rawlings
Editorial-Production Service: Omegatype Typography, Inc.
Composition and Prepress Buyer: Linda Cox
Manufacturing Buyer: Megan Cochran
Cover Administrator: Brian Gogolin
Electronic Composition: Omegatype Typography, Inc.

Copyright © 2001 by Allyn and Bacon
A Pearson Education Company
160 Gould Street
Needham Heights, MA 02494

Internet: www.abacon.com

Between the time Website information is gathered and published, some sites may have closed.
Also, the transcription of URLs can result in unintended typographical errors. The publisher
would appreciate notification where these occur so that they may be corrected in subsequent
editions. Thank you.

Many of the designations used by manufacturers and sellers to distinguish their products are
claimed as trademarks. Where those designations appear in this book, and Allyn and Bacon
was aware of the trademark claim, the designations have been printed with an initial capital.
Designations within quotation marks represent hypothetical products.

Library of Congress Cataloging-in-Publication Data

Kaye, Barbara K.
    Just a click away : advertising on the Internet / Barbara K. Kaye, Norman J. Medoff.
      p. cm.
    ISBN 0-205-31875-4
    1. Internet advertising   I. Medoff, Norman J. II. Title.

  HF6146.I58 K39 2001
  659.13—dc21

                                             00-041625

Printed in the United States of America

10 9 8 7 6 5 4 3 2 1   05 04 03 02 01 00

Contents

Preface

This book describes the Internet's history and Internet advertising's short but robust past and its amazing present. The book also attempts to give some insight into the future of online advertising. The growth of Internet advertising since its 1994 birth has been truly phenomenal. What started out with banners as bland and common as roadside billboards has exploded into a rich-media interactive environment that may soon rival the rabbit hole in *Alice in Wonderland.*

Even though the Internet is a new advertising medium, many of the underlying advertising principles established over time are relevant. The audience must be reached with a message that gains attention and influences attitudes or behavior. Two common phrases heard about success in Internet commerce of all kinds apply directly to advertising: "Eyeballs are golden" and "branding is everything." In other words, the advertising message must be in a place where people can see it—and the more people who can see it, the better. Branding labels products or services in a way that makes them more familiar and therefore somewhat more desirable than unknown products or services. It is so early in the development of online advertising that advertisers are still scrambling to get their message in front of the online public and hoping that their banners are intriguing enough to get that all-important click.

Another goal of this book is to provide meaningful background about how the advertising industry is embracing this new and challenging medium. From its modest beginnings, advertising on the Internet has quickly become a multibillion-dollar business. As advertising professionals become more experienced with using the Internet as an advertising vehicle, we can expect the amount and sophistication of advertising on the Internet to grow vigorously in many ways. Also, the nature of the Internet is such that a full-service ad agency, a national product, and lots of money are *not* requirements for entry or success in Internet advertising. We are still in a period of time when some technical skills matched with some vibrant creativity and Internet savvy can lead to successful outcomes. Hopefully, some people who read this book will use the knowledge contained herein to start their "dot com" fortune.

Just a Click Away: Advertising on the Internet is the first in a series of books that looks at various aspects of mass communication and the Internet. An accompanying Web site will give further information and update material contained in this book.

ACKNOWLEDGMENTS

Creating a high-quality college textbook requires high-quality effort from more people than just the two authors. We gratefully acknowledge the support of the people at Allyn and Bacon who guided us along the way, with special thanks to Karon Bowers and Jennifer Becker. We appreciate the thoughtful suggestions made by the reviewers of this text: Carla Gesell-Streeter, Cincinnati State Technical and Community College; Kathy Brittain McKee, Berry College; and Kartik Pashupati, Florida State University.

Our thanks to research assistants Bryan Nelson and, especially, Moira Tokat-yan, for their help in tracking down webmasters for permission to use the many screen shots taken from the Web. Additional appreciation goes out to Kevin Wheelis, who thought up the title of the book, and to Tyshay Turner, Kim Huff, and Ivey Taylor for their creative input.

A big "thank you" and hugs to James McOmber, Janina and Ted Kowalewski, and Lynn, Sarah, Natalie, and Esther Medoff for their love and patience, as well as for their faith in this project.

Just a Click Away

Chapter 1

Introduction to the World Wide Web and Online Advertising

INTERNET ADVERTISING

The explosive growth of online services, multimedia information, and interactive technology are changing the way goods and services are advertised and sold to consumers. Early on, the Internet was used for sharing scientific and military information and was considered to be "above" commercial endeavors such as advertising and marketing. The emergence of the World Wide Web and online interactive technologies that are inherently appealing to advertisers and consumers has changed the old way of thinking. The advertising community is rushing to get a piece of the global marketplace by establishing itself on the Web.

Ultimately, advertisers have an interactive medium for reaching a prosperous, technologically educated, and savvy target market, but it is also a medium that has led advertisers to rethink traditional marketing efforts and to explore new approaches to advertising and promotion.

The Web's foremost competitor for advertising dollars is television, which is widely acknowledged as the most powerful medium for selling products. While the Web can not yet technologically replicate the excitement, realism, and emotional appeal of television commercials, it is quickly becoming a force to be reckoned with in the advertising world.

This chapter begins with a brief history of the Internet, the World Wide Web, and online advertising. The chapter also provides a look at Internet content and the Internet audience.

HISTORY OF THE INTERNET AND THE WORLD WIDE WEB

The word **Internet** consists of the prefix *inter*, meaning "between or among each other," and the suffix *net*, short for *network*, defined as an interconnecting pattern or system. An *inter-network* or *internet* (small *i*) can refer to any "network of networks" or to any "network of computers" (Bonchek, 1997; Krol, 1995; "Yahoo! Dictionary Online," 1997). The Internet, with a capital *I*, specifically refers to the linked computer network where information is freely exchanged worldwide (Groves, 1997; Pitter, Amato, Callahan, Kerr, & Tilton, 1995).

Although the Internet is commonly thought of as a 1990s phenomenon, it was actually envisioned in the early 1960s. With their eyes on the future, engineers and computer specialists conceptualized sending messages via a system of networked computers. Scientists approached the U.S. government with a formal proposal outlining the need for a decentralized communications network in the event of a nuclear attack. Stanford University was one of a few sites of early Internet development where **Vinton Cerf** and his colleagues researched and developed the communication protocols that would later be used for transmitting information across the Internet. Cerf's pioneering contributions to network technology earned him the title "Father of the Internet."

During the decade of the Cuban missile crisis and the Vietnam war, military strategists were sending experimental transmissions among the armed service agencies through linked computers housed in various locations. In the late 1960s, **ARPAnet (Advanced Research Projects Agency)** was created to advance computer interconnections. ARPAnet soon caught the attention of other U.S. agencies that saw the promise of an electronic network as a means of sharing information among research facilities and educational institutions. In 1969, the first Internet message was transmitted from UCLA to Stanford University. Researchers had hoped to send the entire word *login* through the Internet—the *l* made it and so did the *o*, but after that the computer crashed (Johnson, 1999). Nevertheless, the installation of the network was hailed as a milestone and a UCLA press release noted, "Creation of the network represents a major step forward in computer technology and may serve as the forerunner of large computer networks of the future" (Johnson, 1999, p. 28).

Through the next two decades researchers and scientists continued to expand the Internet's capabilities. The first e-mail message was transmitted in 1972, and it immediately began to dominate network use as it still does today. E-mail also transformed and humanized the concept of networking. Where networking was once thought of as a computer-to-computer connection, after e-mail it was considered a connection between one person and another (Johnson, 1999).

The National Science Foundation was eventually instrumental in designing an expanded network that became the basis of the Internet as it is known today—millions of computers worldwide connected via a vast network that consists of tens of thousands of interconnected subnetworks with no single owner (Pavlik, 1996).

While the Internet was in the later stages of development, **Tim Berners-Lee** and a group of scientists in the European Laboratory of Particle Physics (CERN) were developing a system for worldwide interconnectivity that later became known as the World Wide Web. His efforts in Web development earned Berners-Lee the title "Father of the World Wide Web."

Early Internet information was retrieved by conducting a series of complicated steps to locate data, make remote connections, and download data to a local computer. The process was difficult and time consuming, and it called for an in-depth knowledge of the required commands. Primarily due to its laborious retrieval system, limited accessibility, and scientific content, the public rarely used the Web until 1993, when students at the University of Illinois conceptualized the Web browser Mosaic. Undergraduate **Marc Andreessen** headed the development of **Mosaic** that was designed to simplify Web retrieval through hyperlinks. Mosaic gave users a way to access and share Web-based information without having to master difficult commands or interfaces. For Andreessen's programming work the university paid him all of $6.85 per hour. However, his time and effort soon paid off when Jim Clark, founder of Silicon Graphics, teamed with Andreessen to enhance and improve Mosaic. With Clark's financial backing and Andreessen's know-how, they founded Netscape Communication Corporation in 1994, and Netscape Navigator, an enhanced Web browser was born shortly thereafter. In 1999, Andreessen was named chief technology officer for America Online; more recently he scaled back his AOL responsibilities by positioning himself as a part-time strategic adviser. Andreessen has taken on what he calls a 50-year project to shape the Web into a medium that is bigger than television or telephones (Guglielmo & Spangler, 1999; "Marc Andreessen," 1997; Steinert-Threlkeld, 1999).

Scientists, computer experts, and researchers continue to work on the Internet and the World Wide Web. Vinton Cerf is taking the Internet beyond earthly boundaries and extending it to satellites and into space. Together with fellow researchers, Cerf is developing network protocols for space communication. For one of their first trials they are planning on e-mail wiring the *Mars Surveyor* spacecraft that will blast off every two years beginning in 2001. It could be that, before too long, domain names will have new extenders like *.moon* or *.space* (Stone, 1998).

INTERNET RESOURCES

The Internet is made up of various resources within the World Wide Web—e-mail being the most popular. Online advertising is most prevalent on the World Wide Web and it is also commonly distributed via e-mail, electronic mailing lists, newsgroups, and chat forums.

World Wide Web

The **World Wide Web** stands out from other Internet resources by its ability to present information as text, graphics, audio, and video. The Web's visual and audio display of vast amounts of information has captured the attention of millions of users who effortlessly travel from Web site to Web site with easy-to-use point-and-click Web browsers such as **Netscape Navigator** and **Internet Explorer.** The Web has also piqued the interest of the advertising industry, which recognizes the Web's potential to help it reach its customers.

Electronic Mail

Electronic mail has been around since the early days of the Internet. Along with the Web it is the most popular and widely used Internet application. Some estimates put e-mail use at 400 million people across the globe and claim that in 1999 between 2.2 billion and 7.3 billion messages were sent every day in the United States alone compared with just 293 million pieces of first-class mail ("No Need to Phone," 1998; The Internet Index, 1997, 1999; Sklaroff, 1999).

Electronic Mailing Lists

Electronic mailing lists, often referred to as *listservs,* are sometimes used to send advertising messages because they reach a list of subscribers who have already expressed an interest in a topic. Most lists are based on voluntary membership where individuals subscribe to receive information pertaining to particular subjects such as gardening, dog breeding, golfing, or soap operas. Additionally, many clubs, organizations, special interest groups, and classes use lists as a means of communicating among members. The messages often include information pertaining to certain products and services of relevance to the list audience.

Electronic mailing list subscribers receive e-mail messages sent from the list host and from other members. All subscribers may join in the discussion by posting their responses and messages on the list, or they may choose to correspond with other subscribers on a one-on-one basis.

The term *listserv* is incorrectly but widely used to describe any electronic mailing list. LISTSERV is the brand name of an automatic mailing list server that was first developed in 1986 and is currently marketed by L-Soft International. There are other automatic mailing list servers, such as Majordomo, on the market. These automated list servers manage and distribute messages posted by their subscribers.

Newsgroups/Bulletin Boards

Newsgroups are an alternative to subscription-based electronic mailing lists. **Newsgroups** are topic-specific discussion and information exchange forums open to interested parties. Unlike electronic mailing lists, participants are not required to subscribe and messages are not delivered to individual electronic mailboxes. Rather, messages are archived at the newsgroup site for users to find, access, and respond to at their convenience. Many newsgroups and bulletin boards are housed within Web sites that often carry advertisements in the frames surrounding the comments.

Chat Forums

Chat forums differ from electronic mailing lists and newsgroups/bulletin boards by allowing participants to exchange live, real-time messages. Chatters carry on "conversations" as they would on the telephone, but instead of speaking, participants type in messages to which others immediately respond. There are many chat channels or subject areas for users to select. News.net, for example, is for individuals who enjoy chatting about current events. Chat forums are quickly becoming popular stops on the Internet. It is estimated that by the year 2000 chats will generate an excess of 7.9 billion hours of online use per year (Cleland, 1996). Advertisers are taking advantage of this venue to reach a target group of chatters by placing their promotional messages in chatroom sites.

There are many Web sites that describe Internet resources in further detail. Webopedia (http://webopedia.internet.com) and CNET (http://coverage.cnet.com/Content/Features/Techno/Networks/index.html) are among the most popular.

DEVELOPMENT OF INTERNET ADVERTISING

Online advertising has a short history. Since 1994, Internet advertising has made tremendous inroads into the lives of consumers and marketers. HotWired posted the first banner ad and it also produced the first button ads and first sponsorships.

Box 1.1 ■ FIRST BANNER ADS

Online advertising was born on October 27, 1994, when *HotWired* (http://www. hotwired.com), the online version of *Wired* magazine, signed up 14 advertisers for its online debut. On that day the Web was transformed into a commercial medium. HotWired executives admit they never imagined the profound impact that online advertising would make on the Internet. Figure 1.1 shows the HotWired site as it looks today.

The original idea for selling ad space was loosely fashioned after proprietary services such as America Online (http://www.aol.com) and Prodigy (http://www. prodigy.com) began accepting advertising on their sites. Slow downloading times deterred the use of large ads and long video and audio clips, so HotWired realized its ads needed to be confined to smaller units of space—hence, the **banner ad.** Logos and short messages could be embedded within the banners with the stronger persuasive elements saved for the more detailed hyperlink—usually the advertiser's homepage.

With little idea of how much traffic HotWired would attract or its audience's demographic profile, HotWired set a price of $30,000 for a 12-week commitment and was thrilled when the first advertisers such as MCI, Volvo, and Sprint signed up. Since then, an entire online advertising industry has flourished. Banner ad design, online media purchasing, banner ad tracking, online campaign development, and online audience measurement are just a few of the newly created online advertising functions. HotWired's advertising director had it right when he predicted, "No way will banner ads go away. I think they're going to be part of the Web advertising landscape for a long, long time" (Cuneo, 1996, p. 44; Koprowski, 1999; Williamson, 1996).

The following year saw the emergence and public acceptance of the Web as an interactive medium. Major brands such as Maytag and United Airlines introduced their Web sites and promoted them through banners. Sun Microsystems revolutionized Web advertising with its release of **Java,** a programming language that turns text-only ads into animated ones that play sounds and show videos. Java also baked **cookies**—applications that identify users and track customers' movements around the Web (Koprowski, 1999; Thorson, Wells, & Rogers, 1999).

By 1996, advertisers were experimenting with intermedia promotion—advertising a Web site using traditional media. Advertorials were becoming more lucrative, interactivity was booming, and advertisers were enjoying global exposure and at the same time thinking about localizing through "city sites and specialty niches" (Thorson, Wells, & Rogers, 1999, p. 19). Oldsmobile drove one of the first commercial chatrooms into cyberspace with its Celebrity Circle campaign created to promote interest in the Oldsmobile brand name (Koprowski, 1999).

In 1997, advertisers and marketers were embracing online targeting, while new and improved technologies led to interactive and "smart" banners that brought product information and order forms to consumers' fingertips. Sponsorships hit it big during the year when ZDNet (http://www.zdnet.com) was

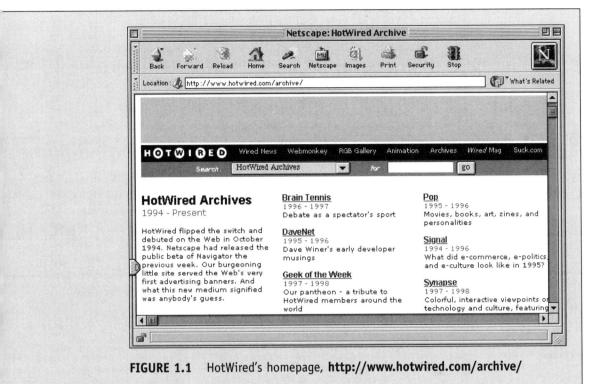

FIGURE 1.1   HotWired's homepage, **http://www.hotwired.com/archive/**

one of the first marketers to give advertisers the opportunity to sponsor site content. Not wanting to get left out of cyberspace, advertising agencies created in-house departments for their online projects and began to think about ways to integrate interactive jobs with their traditional advertising functions. Banners were becoming commonplace and the novelty was beginning to wear off as click-through rates dropped from between 10 to 40 percent in the two preceding years to about 1 percent in 1997 (Koprowski, 1999; Thorson, Wells, & Rogers, 1999; Warren, 1999).

Interstitials, ads that appear in a separate browser window, arrived during the following year and became more common as did other experiential ads that allowed customers to place orders and conduct other interactions directly from the banner. Newspapers banded together to create joint venues for their classified advertisements. **Spam,** unwanted e-mail, was getting out of control and users sought legal help to stem the flow of unwanted ads. Yet, others gladly signed up for online promotions in exchange for free e-mail (Koprowski, 1999; Thorson, Wells, & Rogers, 1999).

More recently, online advertising has evolved into a world of rich-media banners that pop up into their own browser window from which users can order products or get more information. Online advertising is beginning to resemble television commercials as broader **bandwidths** speed the transmission of video images to computer screens around the world. Advertisements are appearing on screens before documents are fully **downloaded** and they interrupt online games and other interactions. Online advertising now comes in many forms from text-only print banners to real-time videos. There is little argument that with each passing year advertising is becoming more and more prevalent in cyberspace.

WHAT IS ON THE WEB AND WHO IS GOING ONLINE

The amount of information on the Web is phenomenal and seemingly limitless. In July 1995, there were an estimated 4 million documents available on the Web. Three months later this number had grown to 8½ million pages, representing a 112 percent increase. The Web was estimated to contain between 16 and 50 million pages of information in 1996; by 1998 the number leaped to 275 to 320 million pages and it is still growing. If all the pages on the Web were printed on paper and laid one on top of the other, the pile would be higher than Mount Everest. The number of online documents is expected to reach a mind-boggling 800 million in the year 2000.

Internet Users in the United States

Estimates of the number of people who use the Internet vary widely. Between 1995 and 1997 the number of United States online users ranged from a low of 5.8 million to about 51 million, depending on the source and the data collection method used. More recent data from RelevantKnowledge and Mediamark Research indicate that in 1998 and 1999 between 57 million and 64 million people in the United States used the Internet. In 1999, Jupiter Communications claimed that in the United States alone there were as many as 90 million Internet users, and the *Computer Industry Almanac* proclaims use has topped 100 million people—40 percent of the population. Many critics claim that Internet user numbers are inflated. As many as 16 million people have not gone online in the past year but they are nevertheless counted in the total number of Internet users ("Cyber Dialogue," 1999).

Before any medium can be considered a mass medium, a critical mass of users must be reached. Generally, critical mass is achieved when about 16 percent of the population has adopted an innovation (Markus, 1987), however, in the case of mass media 50 million users seems to be the milestone and the benchmark used for comparing rates of adoption. The rate of radio adoption crawled along for 38 years before hitting the magic 50 million users, but broadcast television only took 13 years and cable television 10 years to achieve this goal, and it only took the Internet about 5 years to become the newest mass medium. The number of Internet users and the Internet itself are growing so quickly that its life span is often measured in dog years—one Internet year is equivalent to 7 non-Internet years (Neufeld, 1997; "Why Internet Advertising," 1997).

Internet users devote about 13 hours a week to cruising the sites (Johnson & Kaye, 1998). Close to half of these users visit at least one Web site daily and 6 out of 10 open their e-mail every day. The Web has become an integral part of users' lives with over 40 percent reporting that it has become a necessity and over three-quarters claim that it has made their lives better.

Previous claims stated that early Internet users tended to be white males, but more recent studies suggest a demographic shift as the Internet becomes more mainstream. Although in 1996 males accounted for 86 percent of online users, by 1998 women represented 49 percent of all users, and one year later Media Metrix claimed that the ratio hit 50:50. Female Internet users tend to be slightly younger (31.9 years) than their male counterparts (33.4 years). The average income of those who connect is $57,000 to $61,500, almost twice the mean income of offline households. Slightly more than 4 out of 10 Internet users report they are college educated or better, and almost one-third of Internet users hold computer-related jobs, and one-quarter are employed in education ("American Internet User Survey," 1997; Guglielmo, 1999; "GVU's Seventh WWW User Survey," 1997; "GVU's 10th User Survey," 1998; Trager, 1999).

Global Internet Users

The Internet is a global medium and its users are not confined to U.S. borders. In early 1999, an estimated 150 to 180 million people around the world were online and that number is expected to grow to 717 million by the end of 2005. Internet penetration across Europe is expected to double by 2003, and the number of people online in Asia is expected to soar by 600 percent to 90 million by the same year ("64 Percent of Asian-Americans," 1999; "717 Million," 1999; "European Internet Users," 1999). Tables 1.1 and 1.2 detail Internet use by region and nation.

Many countries have witnessed recent surges in Internet use. The number of online users in China rocketed from 2.1 million in 1998 to 8.9 million a year later.

TABLE 1.1   Global Internet Use by Region*

Canada/U.S.	93.6 million
Western Europe/Scandinavia	42.0 million
Asia/Pacific	33.6 million
South/Central America	5.6 million
Eastern Europe	3.8 million
Middle East/ Africa	3.0 million

*Adults over 16 years old, weekly users. (Results could be 15 to 30 percent higher if occasional users were included.)

Source: *Computer Industry Almanac*, 1999.

TABLE 1.2   Top 15 Countries in Internet Use (Year-End 1999)

Rank	Country	Number of Users/ Percentage of Population
1	United States	110.8 million/40.6%
2	Japan	18.1 million/14.3%
3	United Kingdom	13.9 million/23.5%
4	Canada	13.2 million/42.5%
5	Germany	12.2 million/15.2%
6	China	8.9 million/7.1%
7	Australia	6.8 million/36.2%
8	Brazil	6.7 million/3.9%
9	France	5.69 million/9.6%
10	South Korea	5.68 million/12.3%
11	Taiwan	4.79 million/21.6%
12	Italy	4.74 million/8.4%
13	Sweden	3.9 million/48.7%
14	Netherlands	2.93 million/18.5%
15	Spain	2.90 million/7.4%

Source: "Amount of Chinese," 2000; *Computer Industry Almanac*, 1999.

But not all countries are Internet savvy. The Internet is used by only about 6 percent of Croatians and one-quarter of the population is unaware of the Internet's existence. Overall, non-U.S. users are expected to account for 65 percent of the total user population by 2003. Additionally, Datamonitor predicts that by the year 2003, there will be about 545 million Internet users around the world ("Amount of Chinese," 2000; "E-commerce to Top," 1999; "Use of the Net," 1999).

Internet users in other countries are in many ways similar to those in the United States. For instance, American Internet users tend to have higher incomes than non-users. The same trend is evident in Russia, where white-collar professional workers are the most likely to go online and those in the lower income brackets rarely use the Internet. In Great Britain the average household income of Internet users is 80 percent higher than that of non-users. In Northern Ireland, Internet penetration by those with high incomes is six times that of those in the low income brackets ("Fletcher Research," 1999; "One in Eight," 1999).

In South Africa, as in many other countries, Internet use is less frequent among the older population than among those under age 35. Though in the United States the ratio of female to male Internet users is now almost 50:50, in China almost 80 percent of users are male, and in South Africa, Denmark, and Morocco 7 out 10 users are male. However, in Great Britain the gap between the sexes narrows as two out of five users are women, and in Japan and Germany women account for just over one-third of all users ("Amount of Chinese," 2000; "Close to 10 Million," 1999; "Fletcher Research," 1999; "Moroccans Ready," 1999; "Nearly 4 Percent," 1999; "Nearly 50 Percent," 1999; "South African Teenagers," 1999).

The amount of time that non-U.S. users are spending online is increasing as the Internet becomes a larger part of their daily lives; however it still remains low compared to U.S. use. The Chinese spend about 7 hours online each week, Germans 5 hours. British users stay online 4 hours, and the French only spend about 3 hours surfing each week ("Europeans Catching Up," 1999).

In some countries the Internet is taking the place of traditional media use. U.S. Internet users claim that they spend 30 percent less time watching television and 11 percent less time reading newspapers, and time spent reading magazines has dropped by 10 percent. Radio listening has slipped by only about one percent, probably because the radio can be listened to while surfing and Internet radio can be tuned in even while conducting other computing tasks. Internet users in Latin America claim the time they spend watching television has decreased 12 percent and time spent reading newspapers has declined by 10 percent (Kaye & Johnson, 2000; Merli, 1998; Zbar, 1998).

SUMMARY

The Internet's recent explosive growth and popularity have led many to believe that it emerged in the 1990s, but it has actually been in existence for about three decades. For the first 20 or so years of its life, the Internet was used primarily by government and academic researchers for accessing scientific and military information through a series of complicated commands. The public was largely unaware of the Internet's existence until Mosaic burst onto the scene. Mosaic's easy-to-use hypermedia system sparked a surge of interest in the Internet and was the catalyst that transformed it into a free-wheeling computer network where anyone can be both an information provider and an information seeker.

Soon after its birth, the Web was commercialized. Marketers found a new, effective, and interesting way to advertise their products and services. Java programming led to rich-media ads; text-only banner ads made way for eye-catching graphics, animation, audio, and video. Interstitials provide product information, order forms, and other interactive features without moving users from one site to another. The Web is no longer just the newest mass medium; it is also the newest commercial medium.

Every year millions of new users around the world are joining the ranks of the online veterans. The Web has in many ways already become a vital force in people's lives and in the global economy. In the United States alone, the Internet economy is growing in leaps and bounds and shows no sign of slowing in the near future. Companies are anxiously tapping into the Internet market and are reaching for market share through online marketing and advertising efforts.

Discussion Questions

1. In what ways did the Web browser Mosaic spark public interest in the Internet and Web?
2. What communication needs do each of the Internet's resources fulfill?
3. What factors are behind the Internet's quick rise as a mass medium?
4. What are your reasons for using the Internet?
5. Do you consider the Internet a necessity in your daily activities?
6. Do you think the Internet's growth rate will continue? Why or why not?
7. Why do you think some people avoid the Internet?

Chapter Activities

1. Familiarize yourself with Netscape Navigator and Internet Explorer. What are the similarities and differences between the two browsers? Which of the two browsers do you prefer and why?
2. Explore newsgroups and chat forums. Print some of the ads found on these sites and determine the target market and why you think the advertiser chose that particular venue to advertise its products or services.
3. Complete the Internet Values and Lifestyles survey at http://future.sri.com/vals/VALSindex.shtml. This survey asks people about their experiences and uses of the Internet, and collects demographic and consumer data. Explore the ways in which this type of data is useful to the Internet community.

References

15 percent of Slovenians have used the Net. (1999, June 11). *NUA Surveys, e-mail newsletter* [Online]. Available: http://www.nua.ie/surveys

64 percent of Asian American homes online. (1999, December 13). *NUA Surveys, e-mail newsletter* [Online]. Available: http://www.nua.ie/surveys

717 million Internet users globally by 2005. (1999, September 13). *NUA Surveys, e-mail newsletter* [Online]. Available: http://www.nua.ie/surveys

1995 Kilby Young Innovator. (1997). [Online]. Available: http://dc.smu.edu/kilby/Berners.html

Aboba, B. (1993, November). How the Internet came to be. *The online user's encyclopedia.* Reading, MA: Addison-Wesley.

About one in four adults has access. (1996). *1996 National omnibus survey.* University of Maryland Survey Research [Online]. Available: *Alishaw.sccf.ucsb.edu/~survey1/*

American Internet user survey. (1997). *Emerging Technologies Research Group* [Online]. Available: http://etrg.findsvp.com/Internet/findf.html (1998, January 7).

Amount of Chinese Internet users explodes. (2000, January 24). *NUA Surveys, e-mail newsletter* [Online]. Available: http://www.nua.ie/surveys (1999, June 30).

Angell, D., & Heslop, B. (1995). *The Internet business companion.* Reading, MA: Addison-Wesley.

AOL reveals reach of Net. (1998, December 4). *Advertising Age* [Online]. Available: http://adage.com

Berners-Lee, T., Cailliau, R., Luotonen, A., Nielsen, F. K., & Secret, A. (1994). The World Wide Web. *Communications of the ACM. 37* (8), pp. 76–82.

Bonchek, M. S. (1997). *From broadcast to netcast: The Internet and the flow of political information.* Doctoral dissertation, Harvard University [Online]. Available: http://institute.strategosnet.com/msb/home.html

Caruso, D. (1996, January 29). Technology. *The New York Times,* p. C3.

Cleland, K. (1996, September 9). Accipiter latest entrant in race to manage ads. *Advertising Age,* p. 44.

Close to 10 million people online in Germany. (1999, September 20). *NUA Surveys, e-mail newsletter* [Online]. Available: http://www.nua.ie/surveys

CommerceNet and Nielsen Research. (1995). *The CommerceNet/Neilsen Internet Demographics Survey: Executive Summary* [Online]. Available: http://www.commerce.net/information/surveys/Croal, N, & Stone, B. (1996, May 27). Cyberscope: More sites. *Newsweek,* p. 10.

Cuneo, A. Z. (1996, October 21). We had no idea what our audience would be. *Advertising Age,* p. 44.

Cyber dialogue: Study estimates 41.5 million US adults online. (1999, February 8). *NUA Surveys, e-mail newsletter* [Online]. Available: http://www.nua.ie/surveys (1999, June 30).

Datamonitor: 545 million user accounts globally by 2002. (1999, August 16). *NUA Surveys, e-mail newsletter* [Online]. Available: http://www.nua.ie/surveys (1999, August 16).

DeCotis, M. (1999, May 26). The Web and Net are here to stay, trouble and all. *Florida Today,* p. D1.

Ecommerce to top USD1 trillion. (1999, June 28). *NUA Surveys, e-mail newsletter* [Online]. Available: http://www.nua.ie/surveys

Europeans catching up on the U.S. (1999, December 13). *NUA Surveys, e-mail newsletter* [Online]. Available: http://www.nua.ie/surveys

European Internet users. (1999, December 13). *NUA Surveys, e-mail newsletter* [Online]. Available: http://www.nua.ie/surveys

Fahey, T. (1994). *Net.speak: The Internet dictionary.* Indianapolis, IN: Hayden Books.

Fletcher Research: British users fear credit cards. (1999, December 13). *NUA Surveys, e-mail newsletter* [Online]. Available: http://www.nua.ie/surveys

Free access boosts Internet in Italy. (1999, October 26). *NUA Surveys, e-mail newsletter* [Online]. Available: http://www.nua.ie/surveys

Groves, D. (1997). *The Web page workbook.* Wilsonville, OR: Franklin Beadle.

Guglielmo, C., (1999, April 19). Outlook good for online commerce. *Interactive Week, 6* (16), p. 65.

Guglielmo, C., & Spangler, T. (1999, September 13). Andreessen leaves AOL's CTO post. *Interactive Week, 6* (37), p. 10.

GVU's seventh WWW user survey. (1997). *Georgia Institute of Technology's Graphic, Visualization and Usability Center* [Online]. Available: http://www.cc.gatech.edu/gvu/user_surveys/survey_1997

GVU's tenth WWW user survey. (1998). *Georgia Institute of Technology's Graphic, Visualization and Usability Center* [Online]. Available: http://www.gvu.gatech.edu/user_surveys/survey-1998-10/tenthreport.htm l

Half of Korean Net users have bought online. (1999, August 30). *NUA Surveys, e-mail newsletter* [Online]. Available: http://www.nua.ie/surveys

High fees hinder Net growth in Latin America. (1999, December 20). *NUA Surveys, e-mail newsletter* [Online]. Available: http://www.nua.ie/surveys

Hodges, J. (1996, February 26). It's becoming a small World Wide Web after all. *Advertising Age, 67* (6).

Hoffman, D. L, Kalsbeek, W. D., & Novak, T. P. (1996a). *Internet use in the United States: 1995 baseline estimates and preliminary market segments* [Online]. Available: http//www2000.ogsm.vanderbilt.edu/baseline/1995.Internet.estimates.html

Hoffman, D. L, Kalsbeek, W. D., & Novak, T. P. (1996b). *Internet and Web use in the United States: Baselines for commercial development* [Online]. Available: http//www2000.ogsm.vanderbilt.edu/papers/Internet_demos_july9_1996.html

Hyland, T. (1998, February 2). Web advertising: A year of growth. *Advertising Age* supplement, *Online Media Strategies for Advertising,* p. A20.

IDC Research: One quarter of Europeans now online. (2000, January 7). *NUA Surveys, e-mail newsletter* [Online]. Available: http://www.nua.ie/surveys

Internet history. (1996). *Silverlink LLC* [Online]. Available: http://www.olympic.net/poke/IIP/history.html

Internet in Taiwan (1999, December). *NUA Surveys, e-mail newsletter* [Online]. Available: http://www.nua.ie/surveys

The Internet Index. (1997, September 10). *Open Market* [Online]. Available: http://www.openmarket.com/intindex/index.cfm

The Internet Index #24. (1999, May 31). *Open Market* [Online]. Available: http://www.openmarket.com/intindex/index.cfm

The Internet Index #25. (1999, November 30). *Open Market* [Online]. Available: http://www.openmarket.com/intindex/index.cfm

Johnson, B. (1999, August 30). Internet turns the big 30. *Advertising Age, 70* (36), p. 28.

Johnson, T. J., & Kaye, B. K. (1998). Cruising is believing? Comparing Internet and traditional sources on media credibility measures. *Journalism and Mass Communication Quarterly*, (2), pp. 325–340.

Kaye, B. K., & Johnson, T. J. (2000). *From here to obscurity: Media substitution theory and the internet.* Paper presented at the meeting of the Association for Education in Journalism and Mass Communication, Phoeniz, AZ.

The Kelsey Group: Local business market turns to Web. (1999, June 29). *NUA Surveys, e-mail newsletter* [Online]. Available: http://www.nua.ie/surveys.

Koprowski, G. (1999, Fall). A brief history of the World Wide Web. *Critical Mass*, pp. 8–15.

Krol, E. (1995). *The Whole Internet.* Sebastopol, CA: O'Reilly & Associates.

Liberatore, K. (1998, January 20). So what's Yahoo! got to do with it. *MacWorld* [Online]. Available: http://macworld.zdnet.com/netsmart/features/search in.links.html (1998, January 20).

Maddox, K. (1999, February 15). IAB: Internet advertising will near $2 bil for 1998. *Advertising Age*, pp. 32, 34.

Marc Andreessen, co founder of Netscape. (1997). *Jones telecommunications and multimedia encyclopedia homepage* [Online]. Available: www.digitalcentury.com/encyclo/update/andreess.htm (1998, January 21).

Markus, M. L. (1987). Toward a "critical mass" theory of interactive media. In J. Fulk & C. Steinfield (eds.), *Organizations and communication technology* (pp. 194–218). Newbury Park, CA: Sage Publications.

Maudlin, M. L. (1995). *Measuring the Web with Lycos* [Online]. Available: http://lycos.cs.cmu.edu/

McGarvey, J. (1996, January). Latest net survey: 9.5 million active surfers. *Interactive Week*, p. 9.

Merli, J. (1998, October 19). Internet users not foresaking radio. *Broadcasting & Cable, 128* (43), p. 59.

MIDS (1995). *Third MIDS Internet demographic survey (Matrix Information and Directory Services, Austin, TX* [Online]. Available: http://www3.mids.org/ids3/pr9510.html

Moroccans ready to embrace ecommerce. (1999, December 6). *NUA Surveys, e-mail newsletter* [Online]. Available: http://www.nua.ie/surveys

Murray, J. A. E., Bradley, H., Craigie, W. A., & Onions, C. T. (1989). *The Oxford English Dictionary*, 2nd ed. Oxford, England: Oxford University Press.

Napoli, L. (1996). Omnicom boutique investments mark turning point for advertising on the Web. New York Times—CyberTimes [Online]. Available: http://search.nytimes.com/Web/docsroot/library/cyber/week/1018omnicom.html

Nearly 4 percent of Russians now online. (2000, January 10). *NUA Surveys, e-mail newsletter* [Online]. Available: http://www.nua.ie/surveys

Nearly 50 percent increase in Irish Net users. (1999, November 1). *NUA Surveys, e-mail newsletter* [Online]. Available: http://www.nua.ie/surveys

Neufeld, E. (1997, May 5). Where are audiences going? *MediaWeek, 7* (18), pp. S22—S29.

Nine percent of wired Canadians. (2000, January 24). *NUA Surveys, e-mail newsletter* [Online]. Available: http://www.nua.ie/surveys

No need to phone. (1998, January 26). *Newsweek*, p. 15.

NUA's how many online? (1999, January 26). *NUA Surveys, e-mail newsletter* [Online]. Available: http://www.nua.ie/surveys

One in eight homes online in Northern Ireland. (1999, December 6). *NUA Surveys, e-mail newsletter* [Online]. Available: http://www.nua.ie/surveys

O'Reilly survey set U.S. Internet size at 5.8 million. (1995). Sebastopol, CA: O'Reilly Publishing [Online]. Available: www.ora.com/research

Over half of young Estonians are online. (1999, December 20). *NUA Surveys, e-mail newsletter* [Online]. Available: http://www.nua.ie/surveys

Pavlik, J. V. (1996). *New media technology.* Boston: Allyn & Bacon.

Pitter, K., Amato, S., Callahan, J., Kerr, N., & Tilton, E. (1995). *Every student's guide to the Internet.* San Francisco: McGraw-Hill.

RelevantKnowledge ranks the sites. (1998, July 13). *Broadcasting & Cable, 128* (29), p. 51.

Report looks at corporate Web spending. (1999, May 17). *NUA Surveys, e-mail newsletter* [Online]. Available: http://www.nua.ie/surveys (1999, June 28).

Report profiles usage patterns in Middle East. (1999, August 16). *NUA Surveys, e-mail newsletter* [Online]. Available: http://www.nua.ie/surveys

Sklaroff, S. (1999, March 22). E-mail nation. *U.S. News & World Report,* pp. 54–55.

South African teenagers surge online. (1999, December 20). *NUA Surveys, e-mail newsletter* [Online]. Available: http://www.nua.ie/surveys

Steinert-Threlkeld, T. (1999, May 17). Andreessen's next 50 years. *Interactive Week, 6* (20), p. 1.

Stone, B. (1998, August 10). Coming soon: www.newsweek.moon? *Newsweek,* p. 12.

Taylor, C. (1997, July 5). Net use adds to decline in TV use; Radio stable. *Billboard,* p. 85.

Thorson, E., Wells, W. D., & Rogers, S. (1999). Web advertising's birth and early childhood as viewed in the pages of *Advertising Age.* In D. W. Schumann & E. Thorson (Eds.), *Advertising and the World Wide Web* (pp. 5–26). Mahwah, NJ: Lawrence Erlbaum Associates.

Tim Berners-Lee. (1997). *Peking University homepage* [Online]. Available: http://www.pku.edu.cn/on_line/w3html/people/Berners-Lee-Bio.html

Tim Berners-Lee Bio. (1997). *World Wide Web Consortium homepage* [Online]. Available: http://www.w3.org/People/Berners-Lee/Longer.html (1998, January 21).

Trager, L. (1999, March 29). Women even score on Net use. *Interactive Week, 6* (13), p. 16.

U.S. tops 100 million Internet users according to Computer Industry Almanac. (1999, November 4). *Computer Industry Almanac* [Online]. Available: http://www.c-i-a.com/199911iu.htm (2000, February 2).

Use of the Net in Croatia on the increase. (1999, August 23). *NUA Surveys, e-mail newsletter* [Online]. Available: http://www.nua.ie/surveys

Vinton Cerf (1994, June). *Computer Sciences Corporation home page* [Online]. Available: http://www.csc.com/csc_vanguard/bios/u_cerf.html (1998, January 17).

Warren, C. (1999, Fall). Tools of the trade. *Critical Mass,* pp. 22–28.

Web Founder: Tim Berners-Lee. (1996). [Online]. Available: http://www.cytex.com/mitsc/sp96/sp96kcet.htm

Webopedia. (1999). [Online]. Available: http://webopedia.internet.com

Weeks, L. (1998, November 25). On PBS, night of the living nerds. *The Washington Post,* p. D1, col 8.

What a massive Web. (1998, November). *National Geographic.*

What's your daily dose. (1997, November 18). *PC Magazine,* p. 9.

Why Internet advertising. (1997, May 5). *Media Week, 7* (18), pp. S8–S13.

Williamson, D. A. (1996, October 21). Web ads mark 2nd birthday with decisive issues ahead. *Advertising Age Online* [Online]. Available: http://adage.com/search/html (1999, July 16).

Yahoo! Dictionary Online (1997). [Online]. Available: http://www.zdnet.com/yil/content

Zbar, J. (1998, September 21). Internet ground fertile in calmer Latin America. *Advertising Age, 69* (38), p. 38.

Chapter 2

The Internet Economy

ONLINE ADVERTISING

The Internet is hailed as a unique medium that facilitates interaction between information providers, users, buyers, and sellers. Through Web browsers and the Web's hypermedia system, users can easily point and click their way to information and to the purchase of goods and services. The Web is unlike other media in that it presents text, graphics, animation, audio, and video in one venue. Internet technology offers advertisers and marketers the opportunity to interact with their customers through e-mail, newsgroups, surveys, contests and games, and other means of online communication. Advertisers and marketers also have creative and alluring ways to present their messages and products through such forums as online catalogs, product demonstrations, and interactive order forms.

This chapter examines the distinction between online advertising and online marketing and explores the advantages and disadvantages of online advertising from both the advertiser's and consumer's points of view. An overview of the Internet economy is given along with an online purchasing profile and trends in on-line spending and revenue.

ONLINE ADVERTISING AS A MARKETING FUNCTION

Many companies are both marketing and advertising their goods and services on the Web. Though online marketing and advertising are connected, there is a distinction between the two functions. Traditionally, marketing includes pricing, distribution, packaging, and promotional efforts that go beyond paid advertisements. **Marketing** has been defined as "the process of planning and executing the conception, pricing, promotion, and distribution of ideas, goods, and services to create exchanges that satisfy individual and organizational objectives" (Vanden Bergh & Katz, 1999, p. 155).

Advertising is more narrow in scope and has been defined as "nonpersonal communication for products, services, or ideas that is paid for by an identified sponsor for the purpose of influencing an audience" (Vanden Bergh & Katz, 1999, p. 158). This definition excludes other promotional efforts such as personal selling and free demos and contests, which are considered part of the overall marketing process.

Following from the classic definitions of marketing and advertising, an online marketing effort occurs when a company establishes a Web site to sell or publicize its products, interact with customers, promote goodwill, inform the public of larger corporate issues, and satisfy larger corporate goals. This type of Web site fulfills a marketing function because the company is doing more than simply advertising its products and services.

Although **online advertising** is a function of marketing, it focuses on promoting and/or selling a product or service. There is some debate as to what constitutes online or electronic advertising. While addressing the 1996 American Academy of Advertising, an *Advertising Age* editor defined cyberadvertising as "paid advertising on the Web only including linked sites for the paid banners" (Cho & Leckenby, 1999, p. 163). Others, however, conceptualize online advertising as promotional efforts including banners, online catalogs, free samples and trial offers, and other sponsor identifications. Most industry experts, academic researchers, and the authors of this book agree with the former more narrow supposition that online advertising consists of banner ads and other paid promotional messages.

Online advertising, therefore, occurs when a company pays or make some sort of financial or trade arrangement to post its logo or product information with the intent of generating sales or brand recognition on someone else's Internet space. For example, when CDNow pays to place its banner on the *New York Time*'s Web site (http://www.nytimes.com), this is considered Web advertising, whereas CDNow's own Web site (http://www.cdnow.com), where it sells

FIGURE 2.1   CDNow Banner on NYT, **www.nytimes.com/yr/mo/day/world/**

music and videos and offers customers other services, is considered a marketing function. The distinction between online advertising and online marketing is similar to CDNow buying ad space in a local newspaper as opposed to printing a catalog with ordering information; the former is an ad, the latter a marketing endeavor.

The earliest and still most prevalent form of online advertisement is called the **banner ad.** Banners are typically about 6½ inches wide by about one inch high (468 × 60 pixels), though other shapes and sizes are becoming increasingly popular. On the Web, the standard form of measurement is in units called **pixels,** short for *pic*ture *el*ement. A pixel is a single point or dot in a graphic image. Pixels are arranged in rows or columns and packed so closely together that they appear connected. Computer images are made up of thousands (or millions) of pixels. Computer monitors display 72 pixels per inch; thus, one inch equals 72 pixels or dots per inch (dpi).

Traditionally, banners have been little more than an advertiser's logo with some embellishment. To increase consumer interest and to make purchasing easier, banners are more often than not designed as active links to the advertiser's homepage. In other words, the posted banner doubles as a direct connection to the advertiser. For instance, clicking on a CDNow (http://www.cdnow.com) banner

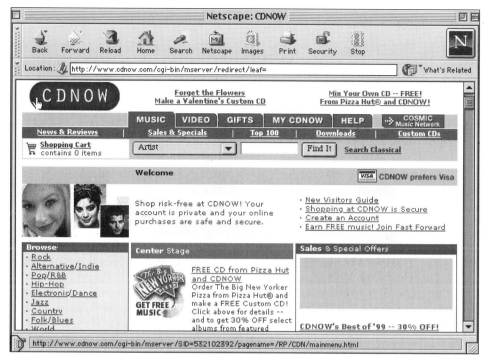

FIGURE 2.2   http://www.cdnow.com/

takes consumers to one of the company's homepages where music lovers can order CDs, videos, and other entertainment fare from the online music store.

BENEFITS OF ONLINE ADVERTISING

Advertiser's Perspective

Advertisers are "private or public companies or organizations that purchase time or space in the mass media to accomplish a marketing or corporate objective" (Aaker, Batra & Myers, 1992, p. 1).

Advertisers are finding that they can use the Web's interactive properties to their advantage. By fine-tuning demographic data and learning from customers' comments, advertising campaigns can be effectively customized to targeted audiences who are changing along with new media. Old models of advertising based on hype and flash no longer carry a strong impact on online-savvy consumers who are responding to ads that are based on information and rational buying appeals.

Advertisers have discovered many benefits in promoting and selling their goods and services online.

Worldwide Marketplace   The Internet and Web serve as a worldwide marketplace that delivers a vast and diverse audience to advertisers. From an advertiser's standpoint, a promotional message placed on a Web page has a potential circulation equal to perhaps hundreds or thousands of newspapers worldwide. Companies that use the Web can sell products to consumers who were previously unreachable, or at least very difficult to reach, using traditional media. For instance, a store or small company may specialize in products unique to its geographic location such as smoked Atlantic salmon or Hawaiian leis. Prior to the Web, advertising these products may have been limited to local media, and sales limited to customers who could physically come into the store or, in some cases, purchase by mail order. By placing advertisements on the Web, companies can now reach out to physically distant customers. Interactive ads display products, tout product features and benefits, and allow online ordering for the convenience of both sellers and buyers.

Targeting Consumers   Advertisers are sending their messages by posting ads on select Web sites and e-mailing product announcements to interested customers. The Web's ability to carry messages to targeted groups is one of its most effective marketing tools. One way to target customers is by geographic location as many customers prefer to purchase local products or they use the Web to gather product information and then shop locally. On Web sites that cater to geographic needs, users enter their ZIP code to bring up local advertisements.

The Web's potential to reach a specific group of customers online has spurred several companies to develop proprietary software to deliver targeted advertising to customers based on their demographic and psychographic profiles, IP address or domain name, type of Web browser, and other criteria. Although these services can be expensive, many businesses feel the expense is well worth it to reach an audience that is most likely to purchase their products.

Through **cookies,** advertisers have yet another way to transmit ads targeted at specific consumer groups. Whenever users fill out personal information on Web pages, cookies basically save data to create customer profiles that companies use to customize their pages and advertisements. A cookie is a message that is sent from a Web server to the user's Web browser (e.g., Netscape Navigator). The browser saves the personal information and sends it to the Web site's server each time a user lands on the site.

The primary purpose of a cookie is to identify users and possibly prepare customized Web pages and ads for them. For example, a sporting goods store could transmit a banner for golf clubs to an older person, whereas a teenager visiting that same site would see an ad for basketball shoes. Although the use of cookies is very controversial because of privacy issues, the function has an enormous potential for target marketing (Waltner, 1996).

Perhaps the easiest way to target online customers is by placing a banner ad on a page or site that will attract the desired audience. For instance, a sporting goods company could buy space on USA Today's (http://www.usatoday.com) online sports section. For example, Worth Global Style Network (http://www.wgsn.com) posted a banner ad on a CNN Interactive (http://cnn.com) style section page that contains an article about the world renowned Kenzo, the Paris-based Japanese designer. Worth Global Style Network "is the world's first fully comprehensive business-to-business online news and information service for the fashion, style and interiors industries" (Worth Global Style Network, 1999). Posting its banner on a style page ensures that it will reach a fashion-interested audience.

Exposure and Run Time   Web ads have longer exposure and run times than ads in traditional media. Traditional media vie for advertising dollars by promoting the advantages of advertising in one medium over the others. For example, one strength of print media is that they have a long shelf life; thus people can read newspapers and magazines any time after publication, even days or years later. Commercial radio spots have the advantage of running many times during the day and capturing an audience's ear with catchy jingles, and television brings life to promotion through video and sound.

What makes the Web unique is that it shares many of the strengths of traditional media. Web ads are visible for as long as the advertisers post them, they can be accessed any time of day and as often as users wish, and they can be printed and used as paper coupons. Web ads can be text-based or they can be more dynamic with graphics as well as audio and/or video presentation. Web ads can be downloaded and stored on users' computers for future reference. These are just a few of the advantages that enhance the Web's allure as a viable advertising medium.

Production Costs   Web advertisements are generally less expensive to produce than ads in traditional media, and the longer exposure and run time makes them even more cost efficient. Ads for traditional media can be expensive to produce— full color separation, audio recordings, video shoots, and other production costs can be very steep. Web ads generally do not require the extensive production techniques as do traditional media, and they can often be designed using digital imaging software such as Adobe Photoshop assisted by **HTML** codes and **JavaScripting.** Low production costs are instrumental in attracting a wider range of businesses with small advertising budgets to the Web.

Advertisers have discovered that by turning to the Web they can reduce print and broadcast production expenses and high distribution costs of direct mailings, as well as reduce their overall advertising expenditures, yet they can still reach their customers.

Updating and Changing Ad Copy   Updating and changing the copy and graphics can be accomplished much more quickly with online ads than with traditional media advertisements. Buying space and commercial time from traditional media, and creating, updating, and changing copy typically require long lead times. Additionally, rigid time constraints and long production schedules often lead to mistakes in broadcast commercials and print ads.

Web advertisements can generally be designed and posted within a relatively short period of time. Web sites tend to have shorter advertising deadlines than the print or broadcast media. Moreover, online ads are easy to correct and change, minimizing the chances of making mistakes.

Competition   Online advertising is becoming a necessary part of doing business. The prestige of online advertising casts a positive image on advertisers and helps new and smaller businesses compete with larger, more established companies. Online, small businesses are not so small. The comparatively low cost of online advertising allows companies with small advertising budgets to compete with companies that have larger advertising resources. The Web closes the gap between large and small enterprises by placing them in the same competitive arena.

Consumer's Perspective

When it comes to making a purchase, there is nothing easier than "letting your fingers do the walking" through the World Wide Web. Like advertisers, consumers are discovering many advantages to using the Web for product information and shopping. Web users benefit from online advertising in many respects. Convenience is presumably the most significant benefit. Almost two-thirds of online shoppers name convenience as the number one reason for purchasing products on the Web. Other reasons for online shopping include easy browsing, product research, and purchasing, as well as pure fun and the novelty of the experience ("Online Shopping Attitudes," 1999). The Web is a single, unified interface for information retrieval and shopping. It is easy for consumers to use the Web to gather product information and to link to a purchase, and, best of all, shoppers do not have to fight for a parking space.

One study found that almost two-thirds of Internet users go online specifically to get information about products to purchase ("AOL Reveals Reach," 1998). Clickable icons yield product information and goods that can be bought by simply entering a credit card number. Additionally, sites like USA Today and the New York Times help Web shoppers connect to products by featuring a sponsor index that provides links to all of the online newspaper's advertisers' home pages. (See Figure 2.3)

Access to Information   When consumers are online, they have access to information that may be difficult to obtain by other means. Additionally, instead of waiting for the mail to be delivered or waiting to call a company during its hours of operation, online information is available immediately, 24 hours a day.

Relevant Information   The Web's ability to target an audience results in customer exposure to online advertising that is relevant to their needs and desires. Customers may be transmitted banner ads that have been targeted to them based on their demographic data or by the keywords they used when searching the Web.

FIGURE 2.3   Graphic of USA Today Sponsor Index, **www.usatoday.com/ads.htm**

For example, on the *Ask Jeeves* (http://www.askjeeves.com/) search site, when the question "Where can I find information about training for a marathon?" was entered, the result screen popped up with a banner ad for Roadrunnersports.com (http://roadrunnersports.com), a Web site featuring running shoes. When "Where can I find a wedding dresses online?" was the question, a WeddingChannel.com (http://www.weddingchannel.com) banner ad displaying a solitaire diamond ring appeared with the list of results. (See Figure 2.4.)

Flexibility   Online ads can be quickly revised to reflect new audience interests and attitudes as well as other changes in the marketplace. Online ads are not as constrained by long lead times and expensive production costs as are those in the print and broadcast media so they can be customized for the audience, and consumers know they are being delivered the latest promotions.

Quick Link to Purchases   Consumers can easily make purchases by simply clicking on a banner ad and following the trail of links to an online order form. In many cases, newer interactive banners allow purchases to be transacted directly from the banner without having to click through a product Web site. Purchasers benefit from the convenience, and electronic orders are processed quickly, cutting the amount of time buyers have to wait before receiving their goods.

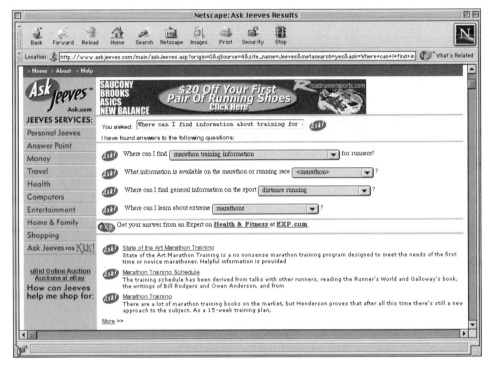

FIGURE 2.4   http://www.askjeeves.com

DISADVANTAGES OF INTERNET ADVERTISING

Although there are many advantages to online advertising to both advertisers and consumers, the very nature of cyberads presents some disadvantages as well. Advertisements and commercials in traditional print and broadcast media are embedded in programs and on pages and thus are intrusive and often unavoidable. Consumers are exposed to persuasive messages in an instant—often even before they have had the chance to turn away from the promotion. Television commercials are generally considered more intrusive than print advertisements, but they do not require greater involvement or attention. Print ads are generally less intrusive but require more cognitive processing.

Although online advertisements, such as banner ads, intrude on computer screens, the persuasive elements are often at least one click away. Consumers must be interested in the product and must click on the banner before being exposed to the sales message. Many products such as automobiles are information intensive and thus are more likely to be clicked on, whereas consumers are less likely to click on a banner for a common household good because the need for information is minimal. Ultimately, consumers have the power to click on some banners while ignoring others.

Banner ads are becoming more technologically sophisticated and many allow purchases to be made directly through the banner. However, banners are still somewhat restricted creatively. Many banners are limited to being nothing more than the equivalent of a roadside billboard. Although many advertisers lean toward banners that lure consumers with animation and movement—the so-called **rich media**—they tend to slow Web page downloading time to a snail's pace.

Despite its abilities to target an audience, the Web is a highly fragmented medium and advertisers face the challenge of placing their message on a site that will draw a large enough audience to make their investment worthwhile. With hundreds of thousands of Web sites and thousands of pages within each site, it is difficult to determine ideal ad placement. **Fragmentation** coupled with inadequate audience measurement techniques limit advertisers' knowledge of how many users are exposed to their message, thus hindering effective advertising buys. To minimize fragmentation and maximize message exposure, many advertisers have struck deals with online services and portals that tend to attract larger audiences. **Portals** are described as online communities, gateways to information, and megasites that provide online services such as e-mail, push services, chatrooms, Web page building tools, interactive games, weather data, and searching, along with other content (McDonald, 1997). Figure 2.5 shows a portal.

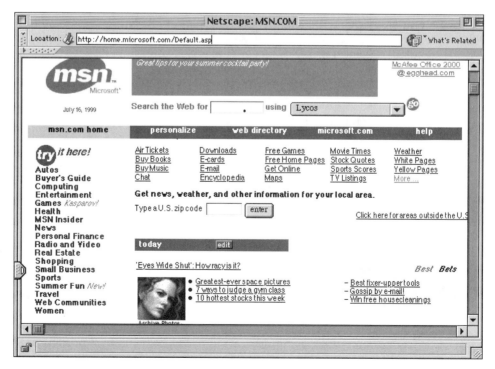

FIGURE 2.5   MSN Home Page (Example of a Portal), **http://home.microsoft.com**

THE INTERNET ECONOMY

Online advertising depends on a healthy Internet economy to draw consumers to the medium and to urge them to purchase products. According to a study conducted by Cisco Systems and the University of Texas, Internet commerce reached $301 billion in 1998, an increase of 174.5 percent from the previous year. Internet commerce is still only a small part of the $8.6 trillion U.S. economy, but it is doubling every 9 months and it is expected to soar to $1.3 trillion by 2003 (Belton, 1999a, 1999b).

Recognizing the Internet economy's growing strength, the U.S. government will begin publishing annual online retail sales figures for the first time. The sales figures for 1998 and 1999 will be available in the year 2000 and will provide affirmation of sales figures collected by research companies ("Internet Grows," 1999). Previously, Internet shopping numbers had been categorized together with catalog sales. As Amazon.com (http://www.amazon.com) founder Jeff Bezos claims, "Internet commerce is not just about selling books, music, and videos online . . . it is an ongoing migration of the $4 trillion global economy onto the Internet" (Taptich, 1999, p. 49).

In the United Kingdom, **electronic commerce (e-commerce)** is expected to bring in over USD 15 billion by the end of 2000—almost double its 1999 figures. Australians are flocking to online stores—their cyber spending is expected to reach USD 5 billion by the end of 2000 and to double to USD 10 billion one year later. Online shopping in Canada still trails the United States and other countries with only an estimated USD 1.1 billion spent in 1999. Overall, it is expected that non-U.S. users will generate just over half of all e-commerce revenue by the year 2003 ("Canada Lags Behind," 1999; "Disparity in Australian," 1999; "Ecommerce to Top," 1999; "UK Ecommerce," 1999).

The Cisco Systems study sectioned the Internet economy into four basic components: (1) Internet Infrastructure—networking, security, hardware, and software, (2) Internet Applications—search engine software and Web server applications, (3) Internet Intermediary—ad brokers, portals/content providers, travel agents, and brokerages, and (4) Internet Commerce—online product sales, fee- and subscription-based companies, travel providers, and online advertising. The estimated revenue of Internet Commerce is $102 billion, one-third of the Internet economy, second only to revenues generated by Internet Infrastructure (Belton, 1999a, 1999b).

Online Shopping Profile

The Internet economy can not thrive without shoppers who are willing to trust the Internet as a reliable and trustworthy shopping outlet. In the United States, between 28 and 40 percent of online users purchased goods on the Web in 1998 with another 21 percent favoring the Web for product and pricing information.

In Western Europe only about 5 percent of Internet users have made online purchases. The British are among the most likely to make an online purchase with just over one-fifth having done so, whereas only about 2 percent of the Spanish have bought something online ("One Quarter," 2000; "UK Ecommerce," 1999).

U.S. cyberpurchasers spent an average of just over $700 buying products online in 1998. In the United States, books, music/CDs, computer software, airline tickets, and clothing led the way in online product purchases. These are also the most-often–bought products in Canada, France, and Great Britain. Additionally, as their online purchasing increases, many online shoppers are making fewer purchases from traditional stores and mail order catalogs ("53 Percent of U.S. Users," 1999; "British Users Fear," 1999; "Canada Lags," 1999; "French Ecommerce," 2000; Guglielmo, 1999; Maddox, 1998a).

While online shopping figures may at first glance seem impressive, on average only about 5 percent of unique visitors to a site become regular customers and only 1.6 percent of the visits result in a purchase ("Online Retailers," 1998). Some sites are better at converting lookers into buyers than others. For example, Amazon.com (http://www.amazon.com), Hallmark Online (http://www.hallmark.com/), and Beyond.com (http://www.beyond.com) all claim that 6 to 8 percent of visitors make a purchase before leaving their sites ("Traditional Marketers," 1999).

Many Internet shoppers are discovering that products purchased online are competitively priced with offline counterparts and there are not many cyber-bargains. The majority of products can be bought for relatively the same price online as offline, only about one in 10 products have a lower purchasing price online, and a scant 1.7 percent actually cost significantly more at an online store ("Report Examines Online," 1999).

Just over one-half of consumers online in the United States report that they would spend more money online if incentives or point schemes such as airline miles, gifts, or electronic cash were offered. Another 37 percent claim that access to real-time advice from online sellers would induce them to open their wallets more frequently. Overall, about half of Internet shoppers report being happy with the experience of cybershopping and claim that the highest priorities in online shopping are convenience, ease of research, competitive prices, and good customer service. Online shoppers are most likely to return to e-commerce sites that give them the best customer service, especially when big-ticket items, such as computers and airline tickets, are involved (Gilbert, 1999; Guglielmo, 1999; "Loyalty Schemes," 1999).

Security is the major obstacle that is keeping shoppers from making more online purchases. Consumers around the world are worried that credit card numbers and personal information will fall into the hands of unscrupulous persons. The inability to handle or try on merchandise, unfamiliarity with online merchants, and time-consuming, difficult site navigation are other reasons that keep consumers from shopping online. Various studies also report that more Internet users would purchase items online if the experience would be as easy and interactive as making a telephone call (Maddox, 1998b).

Online Advertising Spending and Revenue

Many research firms and advertising agencies are tracking online advertising spending and revenue. However, different methods of collecting and analyzing data have resulted in widely varying figures. For example, estimates of Internet advertising revenues for 1998 range from a low of $560 million to about $1.9 billion depending on the source. To make sense of these huge discrepancies, the magazine

Advertising Age has teamed with the research firm eMarketer to analyze the varying spending and revenue figures and to develop new algorithms to provide a more accurate picture of the Internet advertising economy. Even with eMarketer's analyses it still is not possible to provide exact spending and revenue figures so reports offer estimates and projections ("Advertising Age Teams," 1999).

Spending **Online advertising spending** is the amount of money that advertisers pay to place their promotions in cyberspace. Millions of dollars are spent on Web advertising each year, but the amount is still significantly less than that invested in traditional media. After the first half of 1996, Web ad expenditures were only about 10 percent of the amount spent on television network commercials alone, and less than about one percent of the $200 billion spent annually on non-online media advertising in the United States. In 1997, Internet advertising spending grew faster than traditional media advertising (Curme, 1996; "Internet Advertising Becomes Mainstream," 1998; Maddox, 1998a; Napoli, 1999; "U.S. Advertising," 1999; Williamson, 1996).

As Table 2.1 shows, in 1998, U.S. advertising expenditures in all media, including the Internet, increased by 7.5 percent from 1997. Although 1998 ad expenditures topped the growth of the gross national product, the gain was small when compared with the advertising spending on the Internet alone, which jumped 75 percent in one year. Despite the huge increase, online advertising accounts for only half of one percent of the annual U.S. advertising expenditures. The Internet is still a small part of the advertising industry and has a long way to go before becoming a primary advertising vehicle.

In the meantime, traditional media have received a boost from Internet-related companies buying space to promote their services and locations on the Web. Web-based companies such as GoTo.com (http://goto.com/), CNET (http://CNET.com),

TABLE 2.1   U.S. Advertising Spending (1998)

Medium	Spending (Millions)	% of Total Spending	% Change from 1997
Newspapers	$44,292	22.0	+6.4
Magazines	10,518	5.2	+7.1
Broadcast television	39,173	19.4	+6.1
Cable television	8,301	4.1	+14.7
Radio	15,073	7.5	+11.7
Yellow Pages	11,990	5.9	+5.0
Direct mail	39,620	19.7	+7.4
Business papers	4,232	2.1	+3.0
Billboards	1,576	0.8	+8.3
Miscellaneous	25,769	12.8	+7.9
Internet	**1,050**	**0.5**	**+75.0**
Total	201,594	100	+7.5

Source: Coen, 1999.

Deja.com (http://deja.com), Yahoo! (http://yahoo.com), CoolSavings (http://www.coolsavings.com), and E*Trade (http://www.etrade.com) have launched television campaigns to promote their online businesses. In the first nine months of 1998 Internet companies spent just over $322 million advertising their goods and services in traditional media, with $146 million going to television, $81 million to magazines, and $44 million to radio (Coen, 1999; Cuneo, 1999).

U.S. Web ad spending catapulted from $55 million in 1995 to about $175 to $300 million one year later. Forrester Research reports that Internet advertising spending only reached $74 million in 1996. According to eMarketer, cyberadvertising spending has steadily grown from $600 to 650 million in 1997 to between $1.0 and 1.9 billion in 1998. Projections place online spending to continue to climb to $4.2 billion by the year 2000 and to slightly more than double to $8.9 billion two years later ("Advertising Age Teams," 1999; Coen, 1999; "Internet Advertising Becomes Mainstream," 1998; The Internet Index #24, 1999; Maddox, 1998a).

Forrester Research estimates put U.S. online advertising expenditures at $22 billion by 2004 with another $11 billion spent in other countries around the world. By the same year, online advertising spending is estimated to reach USD 5.5 billion in Europe, USD 3.3 billion in the Asia/Pacific region, and USD 1.6 billion in Latin America. Individual countries contribute various amounts to online ad spending and most are expected to increase their expenditures. In France, online ad spending was estimated at USD 47 million in 1999 and is expected to double in 2000 ("Forrester Research: Net Ad," 1999; "France Embraces," 1999; "Net Ad Spending," 1999).

According to Intermedia Advertising Solutions, computer and software companies were the biggest spenders, accounting for almost half of 1998 online advertising dollars with Microsoft leading the way followed by IBM and Compaq (see Table 2.2). When Internet spending is examined by industry category, the ninth ranked retail category was dominated by Barnes & Noble, whose $5 million in online advertising comprised 27 percent of the entire category's spending

TABLE 2.2   Top 10 Internet Advertisers, 1998

1998	1997	Advertiser	Spending (Millions)
1	1	Microsoft Corp.	$34.8
2	2	IBM Corp.	28.5
3	22	Compaq Computer Corp.	16.1
4	9	General Motors Corp.	12.7
5	3	Excite	12.3
6	6	Infoseek Corp.	9.3
7	8	AT&T	9.2
8	16	Hewlett-Packard	8.0
9	42	Barnes & Noble	7.6
10	30	Datek Securities	7.6

Source: "Interwatch" Intermedia Advertising Solutions, as cited in Williamson, 1999.

TABLE 2.3   Top 10 Internet Spenders by Ad Categories, January–September 1998

Category	Spending (Millions)
1 Computers and software	$321.6
2 Financial	59.9
3 Direct-response companies	47.3
4 Media and advertising	35.2
5 Local services and amusements	33.2
6 Automotive, automotive accessories, and equipment	30.4
7 Public transportation and travel	19.2
8 Telecommunications	18.2
9 Retail	18.2
10 Miscellaneous business and technology	11.4

Source: Intermedia Advertising Solutions as cited in Williamson, 1999.

(see Table 2.3). According to the Internet Advertising Bureau (http://www.iab.net), consumer products (including retail, automotive, mail order, toys, and travel), computing, financial services, and telecommunications advertisers account for three-quarters of all online advertising spending.

Revenue   Advertising has become important to the economic viability of the Internet. The past few years have shown that users are reluctant to pay for accessing Web sites. Sites that charge for transactions, such as subscriptions, or for downloading documents have experienced limited success in generating revenue streams. Many Web sites that sell goods and services such as books, CDs, and computer software are still waiting for profits even after being online for a few years. ActivMedia estimates that only about 45 percent of Web sites currently turn a profit with another 20 percent never expecting to be in the black ("Two Thirds," 1999).

Contrary to popular myth, establishing and maintaining a Web site is an expensive venture. Costs of computer hardware and software, Internet connections, and site design can easily soar to millions of dollars just to initially launch a site. Maintenance and trouble shooting fees can tag on several hundreds of thousands of dollars more each year. The average cost of just developing an electronic commerce enabled site is close to $400,000, not including an additional $275,000 for maintenance alone. A poll of the top 100 commerce sites of 1998 revealed that each company spent an average of $8.6 million building, maintaining, and promoting its online site. Although Web transactions and sales hold the promise of making money, in the meantime many online businesses are depending on advertising as a source of revenue (McDonald, 1997; "Report Looks at Changing," 1999; "Sites Invest," 1999; Taptich, 1999).

Online advertising revenue is the amount of money that is brought in by selling ad space on online sites. U.S. online advertising brought in just over $9 million in revenue in 1997. EMarketer has collected 1998 Internet advertising revenue estimates compiled by 13 research firms—the estimates average $1.3 billion in revenue. However, the Internet Advertising Bureau puts the figure at $1.92 billion, surpassing the $1.5 billion spent on outdoor advertising. Several Web analysts forecast that by the year 2000 the Web will reap over $2 billion in advertising revenue ("Advertising Age Teams," 1999; Blundon, 1996; "Internet Advertising Becomes Mainstream," 1998; Maddox, 1998a, 1999; Richtel, 1999).

It is difficult to determine which sites are bringing in the advertising dollars and which are actually seeing a profit. Although online advertising is emerging as a profitable venture, Activmedia reports that only about 16 percent of the commercial sites bring in revenue from advertising. Additionally, it is estimated that online advertising revenue distribution is skewed with about 60 percent of it going to the top 10 most visited Web sites, including the search services (Easton, 1996; Elsworth, 1997; The Internet Index, 1997).

Revenues from online advertising are flowing into many countries around the world. For example, it is estimated that Germany saw USD 82 million in sales generated by online ads in 1999 and this figure is expected to climb to over USD 2.5 billion by 2003 ("German Online Ad Market," 1999).

SUMMARY

There are many advantages to using the Internet as an advertising vehicle. Advertisers have an unprecedented means of reaching a global marketplace and they have the capability of reaching a target group of customers. Means of collecting and compiling demographic profiles give companies insight into their customers, and feedback mechanisms put companies in close touch with the public. Online ads can be posted and changed quickly, and are relatively inexpensive to produce. Small businesses that advertise online can easily compete with large companies with deep pockets.

Internet users are also benefiting from online advertising. Users can ignore banners or they can choose to click on them to travel directly to a product site. Online ads provide an easy path to product information and ordering. The Web empowers consumers, inaugurating new levels of dialog between advertisers and the public. Customers have a direct and powerful voice in product innovation and advertising strategy.

Online advertising expenditures and revenue indicate that the Internet is becoming accepted as an advertising vehicle. Many of the world's leading companies are also the top online advertisers and many are drawing revenue from selling ad space on their sites. All in all, the World Wide Web is a powerful tool that is changing the way goods are bought, sold, and advertised, and it has revolutionized advertising.

Discussion Questions

1. What are the differences between online advertising and online marketing?
2. Do you think banner ads are effective? If so, what kinds of banners work best?
3. How often do you click on a banner ad and why?
4. Do you think that advertisers and marketers should be allowed to use cookies and other customer tracking data?
5. If you owned a small business, would you set up an online shop and would you buy banner space on other sites?
6. How does online advertising help consumers?
7. What are some of the disadvantages of online advertising to the advertisers and to the customers?

Chapter Activities

1. Find an example of a company that has a marketing site and a banner ad on someone else's site. Who is the banner ad targeting and which of the company's products is it promoting? Would you click on the banner?
2. Design on paper a banner ad for a local company. Target the ad to students at your school. Find five Web sites where you could place your ad to reach your audience, and explain why you decided to advertise on these particular sites.
3. Locate five banners ads on the Internet and find their print counterparts. For example, find a banner ad for Dell Computer and also find a Dell Computer ad in a magazine or newspaper. Compare the print and online versions. Do the ads target the Web site or the print medium's audience? Which of the ads do you find more enticing and eye-catching? Is the online or print ad more likely to persuade you to seek more information or buy the product or service?

References

53 percent of US users have bought online. (1999, July 19). *NUA Surveys, e-mail newsletter, 4* (28) [Online]. Available: http://www.nua.ie/surveys (1999, July 21).

@once! Marketing and Advertising. (1995). *@Once home page* [Online]. Available: http://aoma.com/ima.html

Aaker, D., Batra, R., & Myers, J. G. (1992). *Advertising management*. Englewood Cliffs, NJ: Prentice Hall.

Advertising Age teams with eMarketer for research report. (1999, May 3). *Advertising Age, 70* (19), p. S24.

AOL reveals reach of Net. (1998, December 4). *Advertising Age* [Online]. Available: http://adage.com

Beardi, C. (1999, October 18). CoolSavings promotes pink piggy to 'CEO' slot. *Advertising Age, 70* (42), p. 8.

Belton, B. (1999a, June 10). Internet generated $301 billion last year. *USA Today,* p. 1A.

Belton, B. (1999b, June 10). Study: Internet generated $301B in revenue in 1998. *USA Today,* p. 3B.

Blundon, W. (1996, December). Off the charts: The Internet in 1996. *Internet World, 7* (12) pp. 46–51.

British users fear credit cards. (1999, December 13). *NUA Surveys, e-mail newsletter* [Online]. Available: http://www.nua.ie/surveys

Canada lags behind U.S. retail stakes. (1999, September 27). *NUA Surveys, e-mail newsletter* [Online]. Available: http://www.nua.ie/surveys

Cho, C. H., & Leckenby, J. D. (1999). Interactivity as a measure of advertising effectiveness: Antecedents and consequences of interactivity in Web advertising. *Proceedings of the 1999 Conference of the American Academy of Advertising,* pp. 162–179.

Cleland, K. (1996, August 5). Chat gives marketers something to talk about. *Advertising Age,* p. 22.

Coen, R. J. (1999, May 17). U.S. ad growth hits 7.5% in '98 to outpace GNP. *Advertising Age, 70* (21), p. 30.

Cuneo, A. Z. (1999, January 25). "Dot coms" are hot growth opportunity for "old" media. *Advertising Age, 20* (4), pp. 3, 58.

Cuneo, A. Z. (1999, November 1). Yahoo! TV ads connect the brand with shopping. *Advertising Age, 70* (45), p. 62.

Curme, O. (1996, July, 15). Web commerce in transition—Today's Web advertising will be replaced by a broader business model. *Information Week,* p. 94.

Damashek, H. (1996, September 4). A tool belt for Web publishers and advertisers. *Advertising Age,* p. s32.

Disparity in Australian Internet figures. (1999, October 18). *NUA Surveys, e-mail newsletter* [Online]. Available: http://www.nua.ie/surveys

Ducoffe, R. (1996). Advertising value and advertising on the Web. *Journal of Advertising Research, 36* (5), pp. 21–33.

Easton, J. (1996, December). Hidden revenue hotspots. *ZD Internet Magazine.* pp. 99–106.

Ecommerce to top USD1 trillion by 2003. (1999, June 28). *NUA Surveys, e-mail newsletter* [Online]. Available: http://www.nua.ie/surveys

Elsworth, P. C. T. (1997, February 24). Internet advertising slowly. *New York Times,* p. C5.

Executive guide to marketing on the new Internet. (1996). *Industry.Net home page* [Online]. Available: http://www.industry.net/guide.html

Forrester Research: Net ad spending to hit USD33 billion by 2004. (1999, August 16). *NUA Surveys, e-mail newsletter* [Online]. Available: http://www.nua.ie/surveys (1998, April 26).

France embraces online advertising. (1999, November 23). *NUA Surveys, e-mail newsletter* [Online]. Available: http://www.nua.ie/surveys

French ecommerce revenue to double. (2000, January 24). *NUA Surveys, e-mail newsletter* [Online]. Available: http://www.nua.ie/surveys

German online ad market to surge in value. (1999, August 10). *NUA Surveys, e-mail newsletter* [Online]. Available: http://www.nua.ie/surveys

Gilbert, J. (1999, September 13). Customer service crucial to online buyers. *Advertising Age, 70* (38), p. 52.

Gilbert, J. (1999, November 1). Deja.com comes of age with 1st TV campaign. *Advertising Age, 70* (45), p 32.

Guglielmo, C. (1999, April 19). Outlook good for online commerce. *Interactive Week, 6* (16), p. 65.

Hawkins, D. T. (1994, March). Electronic advertising on online information systems. *Online,* pp. 26–39.

Hawn, M. (1996, April). Stay on the Web: Make your Internet site pay off. *MacWorld,* pp. 94–98.

Hoffman, D. L., & Novak, T. P. (1995). Marketing in hypermedia computer-mediated environments: Conceptual foundations [Online]. Available: http://www.2000.ogsm.vanderbilt.edu

Internet advertising becomes mainstream. (1998, April 14). *NUA Surveys, e-mail newsletter* [Online]. Available: http://www.nua.ie/surveys (1998, April 26).

Internet grows by leaps and stumbles. (1999, February 6). *The Orlando Sentinel,* p. C1.

The Internet Index. (1997, September 10). *Open Market home page* [Online]. Available: http://www.openmarket.com/intindex/index.cfm

The Internet Index #24. (1999, May 31). *Open Market home page* [Online]. Available: http://www.openmarket.com/intindex/index.cfm

Loyalty schemes a draw for e-consumers. (1999, July 5). *NUA Surveys, e-mail newsletter* [Online]. Available: http://www.nua.ie/surveys (1999, July 8).

Maddox, K. (1998a, April 6). Internet ad sales approach $1 billion. *Advertising Age,* pp. 32, 34.

Maddox, K. (1998b, October 26). Survey shows increase in online usage, shopping. *Advertising Age,* pp. S6, S34.

Maddox, K. (1999, February 15). IAB: Internet advertising will near $2 bil in '98. *Advertising Age, 69* (44), p. 38.

Mand, A. (1999, May 31). The quest for reach. *Brandweek, 40* (22), pp. 34–36.

McDonald, S. C. (1997). The once and future Web: Scenarios of advertisers. *Journal of Advertising Research, 37* (2), pp. 21–28.

Napoli, L. (1999, February 10). Quarterly Internet ad revenues double. *The New York Times on the Web* [Online]. Available: http://www.nytimes.com/search (1999, February 19).

Net ad spending to hit USD33 billion by 2004. (1999, August 18). *NUA Surveys, e-mail newsletter* [Online]. Available: http://www.nua.ie/surveys

One quarter of Europeans now online. (2000, January 17). *NUA Surveys, e-mail newsletter* [Online]. Available: http://www.nua.ie/surveys

Online retailers share inside view. (1998, November 25). *Interactive Week Online* [Online]. Available: http://www.zdnet.com/intweek/stories (1998, December 4).

Online shopping attitudes. (1999, May 18). *USA Today*, p. D1.

Report examines online luxury goods market. (1999, July 19). *NUA Surveys, e-mail newsletter, 4* (28) [Online]. Available: http://www.nua.ie/surveys (1999, July 21).

Report looks at changing face of the Net. (1999, March 29). *NUA Surveys, e-mail newsletter* [Online]. Available: http://www.nua.ie/surveys (1999, July 2).

Richtel, M. (1999, May 4). Mixed news at online ad conference. *The New York Times on the Web* [Online]. Available: http://search.nytimes.com/search/daily/ (1999, June 22).

Riedman, P. (1998, July 20). GoTo.com kicks off $6 mil ad campaign. *Advertising Age, 69* (29), p. 23.

Sites invest USD 8.6 million on marketing. (1999, May 17). *NUA Surveys, e-mail newsletter* [Online]. Available: http://www.nua.ie/surveys (1999, June 30).

Taptich, B. E. (1999, March). Less than zero. *Red Herring*, pp. 47–50.

Traditional marketers catch on to E-commerce. (1999, July 12). *Business Wire.*

Two thirds of B-to-B sites to turn a profit. (1999, July 5). *NUA Surveys, e-mail newsletter* [Online]. Available: http://www.nua.ie/surveys (1999, July 8).

U.K. ecommerce to top USD15 billion by 2000. (1999, September 6). *NUA Surveys, e-mail newsletter* [Online]. Available: http://www.nua.ie/surveys

U.S. advertising during the 20th century. (1999). *The Advertising Century (Advertising Age* special issue), p. 126.

Vanden Bergh, B. G., & Katz, H. (1999). *Advertising principles.* Lincolnwood, Illinois, NTC Business Books.

Waltner, C. (1996, March 4). Going beyond the banner with Web ads. *Advertising Age, 67,* p. 22.

Webopedia. (1999). [Online]. Available: http://webopedia.internet.com

Williamson, D. A. (1996, September 2). Web ad spending at $66.7 million in 1st half. *Advertising Age, 67* (36), p. 10.

Williamson, D. A. (1999, May 3). Marketing on the Web shifts toward mainstream. *Advertising Age, 70* (19), p. s8.

Worth Global Style Network (1999). *Homepage* [Online]. Available: http://www.wgsn.com/whatiswgsn/whatiswgsn.html (1999, September 15).

Chapter 3

Online Ads: What They Are and How They Are Priced

▪ TYPES OF CYBERADS

Online advertising is often thought of as just plain old banners, but there are really many variations of banners and other types of advertising. Banners have evolved from being static logos to being rich-media sellers of products in the form of interstitials and pop-ups. Additionally, online ads are beginning to mimic television in their appearance as Webmercials, video banners, and infomercials. Additionally, online coupons, advertorials, and classifieds look a lot like their print counterparts.

In 1998, banner ads accounted for just over half (53 percent) of all online advertising, followed by sponsorships (30 percent), and interstitials (6 percent). Another 11 percent consisted of other forms of ads (Maddox, 1999). EMarketer, a New York research firm, predicts by the year 2001 only about one-quarter of all online ads will be banners as they are known today, the rest will be in a form made possible by some technology that has not yet been created (Napoli, 1999).

This chapter describes the different types of online ads. It also takes its readers on a journey through pricing models and the issues surrounding online advertising rates.

Banner Ads and More

Banner ads are still the most common form of online advertising. Banners can be found on all types of Web sites, in chatrooms, as part of newsletters, and in other Web venues, and they take many forms—some are embedded as part of online games, others are posted as coupons. Advertisers have a variety of buys and can certainly find the online outlet that is most appropriate for their product or service.

Plain old banners have gotten a bad rap for being too boring and unattractive and for doing nothing to build sales or audience. In response, advertisers and industry experts have closely scrutinized the performance of banners and, much to their surprise, found that even modest banner campaigns can significantly boost their audience size. One of Nielsen's NetRatings' reports released in late 1998 claims a relationship between sites that consistently advertise online and an increase in the site's audience size. For example, Microsoft's Network's CarPoint site (http://carpoint.msn.com) realized a 44 percent gain in audience over a two-month period in 1998 when it was running a banner campaign for the site. GoTo.com (http://www.goto.com) had a similar success when it increased its number of Web banners by 53 percent (to 237 million impressions) from June to July 1998. During the same time period its number of site visitors increased 24.9 percent to 3.1 million. These examples represent major online endeavors and thus may not be representative of all online campaigns, but NetRatings claims that consistent advertising brings audience growth. A Jupiter Communications analyst called banners "the whipping boy of the Internet," adding, "But our take is that banners do certain things very well—like drive traffic—and that over time, they

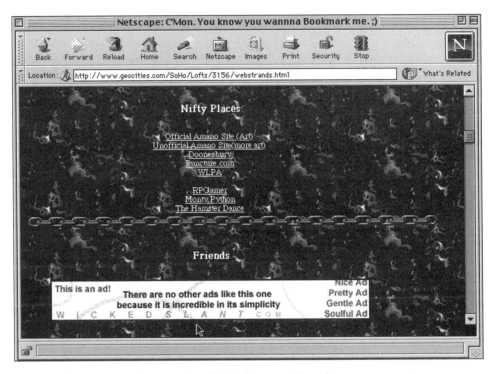

FIGURE 3.1   Plain Old Banner for Wickedslant.com Posted at
http://www.geocities.com/SoHo/Lofts/3156/webstrands.html

will become the workhorse of the online media buy" (Tedeschi, 1998). Figure 3.1 presents a plain banner.

Rich-Media Ads   Banner ads can consist of text-only content or may be what is termed a **rich-media ad.** Rich media is not a type of ad per se but describes how ads are designed. Different from text-only banners, *rich media* refers to ads that are animated, contain audio or video, or just flash, blink, or make weird sounds. Rich-media ads are typically characterized by the ad's size measured in **kilobytes.** The more animation, video, and audio, the more kilobytes consumed. Most ads beyond the 10- to 12-kilobyte size of a conventional banner are considered rich-media. For example, a 1-800-Flowers ad that promoted Mother's Day in 1999 ate up 45 kilobytes, but it allowed users to place their orders right from the ad without leaving the site the ad appeared on. The larger the size of the ad, the longer it takes to download, and the greater the odds that users will click away out of impatience. After many complaints, sites such as Yahoo! limit their banners to about 12 kilobytes, which has become an informal standard. Rather than limiting ad sizes, some sites offer **opt-in rich media** where standard banners download quickly but users can click to see the rich-media version if they do not mind the wait (Maddox, 1998a; Tedeschi, 1999).

Rich-media ads can be a bit distracting with so much lively content packed in a small space. Putting several of those ads on one page may draw visitors' eyes away from page content to the ads. The advertisers love it, but the content providers may be less than enamored. A CBSMarketwatch.com vice president complained, "I had one page where there was a plane flying in and landing on a banner ad, an interstitial pop-up, and four or five buttons. Not only was I assaulting the user who was coming to read the content; in the meantime, I've completely diluted the page" (Napoli, 1999).

All these bells and whistles are not always needed to increase response. A simple audio component alone may be enough to increase interest and interaction. RealNetworks tracked the results of a Coolsavings.com (http://www.coolsavings.com) campaign in which the coupon company ran identical banner ads, except one banner contained a RealAudio button where clickers could hear a 20-second product message. The nonaudio version of the banner was posted for one week and was followed by a one-week placement of the audio-enhanced banner. The nonaudio banner produced a .61 percent click response rate and generated nine customer sign-ups per day. The audio enhanced banner drew a 1.7 percent **click-through** (percentage of users who clicked on the ad) and 150 sign-ups per day. The audio banner increased click-throughs by 190 percent and sign-ups by a whopping 1,600 percent.

There are several basic technological barriers to rich media: They are expensive to produce, not everyone knows how to create the ads, and not every Web site can support the technology. A typical rich-media ad can cost $3,000 to $5,000 to create; if several different versions of the ad are produced, the costs can be much higher. In any case, the cost of a rich-media ad exceeds the average $1,000 price of producing a non–rich-media banner (Tedeschi, 1999).

Pop-Up Ads

Pop-up ads are named as such because they pop-up on users' screens unexpectedly. Interstitials and superstitials are types of pop-up ads that require users to either close the window in which the ads appear or to further explore the ad.

Interstitials   Online users can not help but notice **interstitials** that pop up on their screens. The word *interstitial* means *in between.* Thus the ad appears in between pages or sites. Interstitials pop up in a separate browser window that almost completely covers the screen and appears for several seconds until a site or page is fully downloaded. When customers click on an interstitial, they are usually taken to the advertiser's Web site or they may conduct some type of interaction such as online ordering directly from the interstitial (Hansell, 1998).

Interstitials often include rich-media components that may contain surveys, direct response mechanisms, dialog boxes, audio, and animation. If users do not close the interstitial/pop-up window within a a few seconds, they are sometimes automatically whisked through cyberspace to the advertiser's home page. Figure 3.2B shows an interstitial.

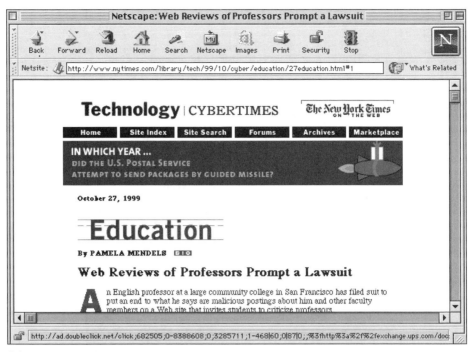

(A)

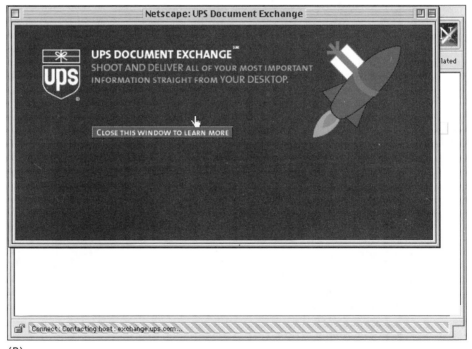

(B)

FIGURES 3.2A, 3.2B, 3.2C UPS Banner Ad on New York Times Online. Banner leads to pop-up ad, which leads to UPS document exchange page.

(continued)

(C)

FIGURES 3.2A, 3.2B, 3.2C   *(continued)*

Advertisers love the fact that users have to close the pop-up window to get back to their destination Web site because it means that customers have seen the ad and have taken an action. Users, however, are not so enamored with these ads that dominate the screen and interrupt their online sessions. Additionally, the way interstitials are delivered further delays users' access to content. An interstitial begins streaming at the same time a Web page is trying to load, delaying access to the new page. To minimize this delay, interstitials are limited in size and the type of multimedia applications they can use (McCloskey, 2000).

Superstitials   Superstitials are closely related to interstitials and they also appear in a separate browser window that pops up between pages or sites. Superstitials were developed by the Unicast Corporation, which has trademarked the name *Superstitial* (Tedesco, 1999).

Superstitials are pre-**cached** (pre-stored) as opposed to being streamed. Superstitials are often referred to as "polite" ads because they only play when initiated (such as by clicking the mouse) by users and only when fully downloaded. Superstitial delivery works by caching a code into the user's browser. The code remains dormant until all editorial content is finished downloading. Only when a page is fully loaded will the superstitial begin downloading in the background. In other words, a new browser window will not initially appear when a user first lands on a site containing a superstitial. But while the user is moving around the site and the editorial content is being fully downloaded, the superstitial will start downloading. Once it is fully downloaded, the superstitial will then pop up in a separate browser window. Users, thus, do not experience the same delay problems with superstitials as they do with interstitials, which are typically streamed along with content (Folb, 1999).

Just as the name implies, superstitials offer more of a presence than interstitials. Superstitials dazzle eyeballs with commercial-length animation, graphics, interactive transactional engines, and almost television-quality video. "Superstitials are the richest of the rich" (Folb, 1999). Superstitials can be any size on the screen and use up to a self-imposed 100K in memory. Superstitials also support rich-media technologies such as **Java,** Flash, and **HTML** as well as long-form animated **GIFs.** Superstitial technology allows broadband-type delivery in an interstitial arena, meaning that ads are looking more and more like television commercials (Folb, 1999).

Although many users find superstitials less annoying than interstitials, they still resent the interference presented by pop-up ads. However, it is unlikely that advertisers are going to shy away from superstitials, especially after recent studies have shown that users are drawn to superstitials' attention-getting presentations and they are more likely to interact and click on them than interstitials. Click-through rates for superstitials range from 7 to 40 percent (Folb, 1999). Users rate superstitials more positively than interstitials and they are twice as effective in creating ad awareness. Moreover, half of the users who see a superstitial either interact with the ad or view the entire message before clicking away, and users are twice as likely to purchase a product or service after viewing a superstitial than an interstitial ("Millward Brown Interactive," 1999; Folb, 1999).

Extramercials

ZDNet (http://www.zdnet.com) has a new approach that gives its advertisers more space to promote their products and services. ZDNet sells what it has dubbed an **extramercial,** which is a three-inch space to the right of the screen that is usually not visible unless users scroll sideways or their monitor resolution is sized at 832×624 or smaller. On many Web sites, the space remains empty as the page content is often built to fill screens with 640×480 resolution. When a viewer clicks on the "expand ad" button at the top of the column, a full-column ad appears. Although ZDNet charges a premium over its basic banner rate for the extramercial, it acknowledges that up to half of its visitors may not be able to see the extra column unless they have reduced the size of the browser window (Johnson, 1998) (see Figure 3.3).

FIGURE 3.3   ZDNET Extramercial, **http://www.zdnet.com/**

Video Banners

Video banner ads (v-banners) are banners that contain a video clip and thus tend to be clicked on more frequently than nonvideo banners. The first v-banner was a promotion for Goldwin Golf posted on *Golf Magazine*'s site. The v-banner featured a three-second looping video of golfer Nick Price endorsing the company's line of golf clubs. About 5.8 percent of visitors clicked-through the v-banner compared to only 1.8 percent who clicked on a similar but nonvideo Goldwin banner. Even though the Goldwin v-banner's 5.8 percent response represented a 250 percent increase over traditional banners, advertisers are concerned about the low rate of response in general ("Improving Their Swing," 1998).

Video banners are very common and are not as complex as some interstitials and superstitials. They often take up less bandwidth and users do not have to bog down their systems with complex extensions and files such as Shockwave. Often, a basic free version of RealPlayer is enough to jump-start video banners. RealNet (http://www.realnetworks.com) posts examples of video banners.

Webmercials

Webmercial is another new cyberterm that is quickly becoming part of everyday language. Webmercials have "the look and feel of a television commercial," and last anywhere from about 5 to 25 seconds. Webmercials grab a captive audience as they pop up when viewers are waiting for a page to download or a search to be completed ("Web Clutter, etc.," 1999).

True webmercials that come on automatically could be the next wave of on-line advertising. "Instead of having a banner ad that takes up part of the screen all of the time, these take up all of the screen part of the time" (Richtel, 1997). Until technology catches up, most webmercials are in the form of a video clip within a window of some sort where users must actively click on a RealPlayer-type application to begin the promotion.

Berkeley Systems has an online interactive version of its computer game You Don't Know Jack (http://www.won.net/channels/bezerk) that is based on its CD-ROM quiz show where game rounds are accompanied by lively, sarcastic voice-overs. After every round of questions a minicommercial appears on the screen. Several years ago, game players were treated to the 7-Up jingle accompanied by video and animation.

While webmercials are certainly attention grabbing, some critics fear that Web users resent being held captive for these 10-to-15–second spots, especially if they have to wait for them to download. Webmercials go against the grain of the Internet, which is supposed to allow users to quickly pick and choose the information they wish to see and not force them to watch commercials. As an industry executive once said, "Just because we face the equivalent of a television screen, doesn't mean we have to have a television model. This is another way of forcing the television model on the interactive medium" (Richtel, 1997).

Advertorials/Infomercials

Consumers have been caught off guard for years by **advertorials** and **infomercials** that blur product information with sales pitches—and now these formats have made their way online. Traditionally, advertorials are copy-only print ads that are designed look like a news story. Readers often mistake a sales message and product information as a news article. Fortunately, newspapers label their advertorials, box them off from editorial copy, and set them in a unique type font.

Infomercials are the broadcast counterpart to advertorials. Infomercials can be of any length from 2 minutes on up to an hour and even longer. Infomercials are basically long commercials that are produced to look like a television program.

The television infomercial and print advertorial formats are being modified to fit the online environment. The multimedia company Narrative Communications (http://www.narrative.com) developed what it calls Enliven technology that produces compelling animation, colorful graphics, and interactivity to create jazzy infomercials that can disguise sales pitches as product information. Advertorials/infomercials are especially designed to attract the attention of Web users who may pay little attention to banner ads.

Traditional media are held to editorial standards that require them to differentiate between advertising and editorial content. Clearly distinguishing ads from editorial content in print publications and infomercials from television programs, alerts readers and viewers that the content is advertiser-produced. On the Web the distinctions may not be so clear, especially to novice users. It is crucial that webmasters maintain a Web site's integrity by clearly marking and separating advertising messages from editorial content. Advertorial/infomercial pages should be designed so that consumers are aware of the source of information and possible content bias (Cleland, 1996). CNN Interactive (http://www.cnn.com) clearly states its advertorial policy and accepts advertorials only if the content is clearly identified as the advertiser's and not CNN's.

More troubling to many online users, especially parents, is the blurring of content and advertising aimed at children. Web sites such as Nickelodeon's Nick-at-Nite (http://www.nick-at-nite.com), Pokemon World (http://www.pokemon.com), and the Cartoon Network (http://www.cartoonnetwork.com) draw more than 15 percent of their audience from children under the age of 12. Overall, there are more than 50 companies creating online sites for 5-to-17-year-olds (Mendels, 1997). Children log on to these youth-oriented sites to play games, solve puzzles, interact with their favorite characters, and get involved with other cool activities. Little do they know that they are being fed advertising messages and that when they answer game questions or interact they are providing the company with marketing information. Activists and parents are calling on sites to set limits on their advertising and to make it clear when information will be used for marketing purposes. For example, banner ads on the Nick-at-Nite site are labeled as such. KidsCom places its Ad Bug wherever advertisements appear on its site (see Figure 3.4). Many would also like to see some commercial-free Web areas where children have access to information and entertainment without being bombarded with advertising (Austen, 1999) (see Figure 3.5).

FIGURE 3.4 Found on the KidsCom Site, the Ad Bug® Is a Fun Way to Alert Children to Advertising Content, **http://KidsCom.com**

FIGURE 3.5 Sesame Street Page with Labeled Ad, **http://www.sesamestreet.com/**

The online audience is already weary of deceptive content and the overcommercialism of the Web so they are not very receptive to cyberinfomercials. Many users respond unfavorably and resent advertising masked as editorial content or helpful product information. Negative attitudes toward infomercials are causing many webmasters to rethink and resist accepting advertorials/infomercials on their sites (Wingfield, 1997).

ADVERTISING RATES

Inconsistent pricing and imprecise means of knowing just how many people are visiting sites and seeing ads make it difficult to compare advertising costs with those of traditional media and to calculate the value and effectiveness of cyberads. Even large companies that allocate vast sums of money to promote themselves in traditional media have been slow to commit ad dollars to the Web.

Coca-Cola and Procter & Gamble have invested very little money in online advertising and view their online efforts as experimental (Elsworth, 1997). At the 1998 meeting of Adtech, a Procter & Gamble vice president claimed, "The current state of Web advertising just isn't effective enough to warrant any truly meaningful investment from us" (Maddox, 1999).

In contrast, AT&T, IBM, General Motors, Microsoft, and Hewlett-Packard are just a few of the heavy hitters who are enthusiastically investing in Internet advertising. Like many other advertisers, they are concerned about the cost of online advertising. Measuring what advertising on the Internet is worth and determining how much it should cost is a subject of debate. Internet ads can be priced using various means currently employed by print and broadcast media; some of these measures have been modified and adapted to the online environment. But the fact that these means of pricing ads can be used does not necessarily mean that they should be, or that they are the proper way to determine the cost of online advertising.

Cost per thousand, click-through rates, time spent listening/viewing, size-based pricing, and cost per transaction fees are just a few of the ways online advertising is being priced. While each method has its advantages and disadvantages, many people argue that one method should be selected and applied uniformly for all ads, but others argue that each entity that sells space should select the pricing method that works best for its outlet and for its advertisers.

Cost per Thousand

Cost-per-thousand (CPM) impressions are typically used to sell print and broadcast media and they are one of the most effective means of comparing the price of advertising across different media. CPMs are commonly used to compare the cost of advertising in newspapers versus television, or radio versus magazines. The formula for computing CPMs can be adapted to any medium.

CPM is calculated by dividing the cost of an advertisement by the number of individuals or households (in thousands) that are reached. For example, if a newspaper charges $13,000 for a full-page advertisement and has 400,000 subscribers, the CPM is as follows:

CPM = $13,000/400 = $32.50 per thousand

Compare $32.50 per thousand to a radio station that charges $2,500 for a commercial that reaches 70,000 listeners:

CPM = $2,500/70 = $35.71 per thousand

A Web site that will be visited by 300,000 viewers may charge $12,000 for a banner ad:

CPM = $12,000/300 = $40 per thousand

In these examples, the radio station may charge less money ($2,500) for its commercial, but it is a more expensive purchase ($35.71 CPM) than the newspaper because it reaches a smaller audience. Although the newspaper ad may seem more expensive ($13,000) at first glance, it is actually the least expensive ($32.50 CPM) of the three options. Whereas the banner ad costs less ($12,000) than the newspaper ad, it is actually a more expensive purchase ($40 CPM) when the number of viewers/readers is considered.

Early on, Web advertising was charged by flat monthly or quarterly rates, but these have since given way to more traditional rate structures. Netscape Communications Corporation (http://www.netscape.com) started out by charging flat fees but later changed to a cost per thousand model (CPM). Netscape's prices vary from $5 to $50 per thousand impressions depending on whether ads are placed on the Netscape home page, an internal site page, or a Netscape newsletter page. USA Today (http://usatoday.com) posts some flat rate charges but mostly relies on CPM. For example, charges for its marketplace ads are based on a $50 CPM.

Though media planners take CPM into consideration when comparing costs, they often place more emphasis on audience demographics, the advantages of each medium, and the medium's ability to reach a targeted audience. Ad space purchase decisions are often based on a combination of factors and not just on the cost of reaching the total audience alone (Bovee & Arens, 1986; Head, Sterling & Schofield, 1994).

In the preceding example, the banner ad's cost per thousand ($40) is higher than the newspaper's ($32.50), but direct comparison may be misleading because the banner may be on a Web site that reaches a select target audience whereas the newspaper ad reaches a more general audience. The same can be said when comparing television to the Web. Although Web CPMs tend to run 66 percent higher than television CPMs, Web ads reach an identified audience whereas network television reaches an untargeted mass audience. Online advertising costs $40 to $100 dollars to reach 1,000 adults, but it costs only about $30 to reach the same number of adults with a television commercial aired during prime time (The Internet Index, 1997; Rebello, Armstrong & Cortese, 1996).

In many cases, dollar for dollar, Web advertising can be more expensive than television or newspapers, though recently CPMs seem to be trending downward. The Internet can actually be the more cost efficient buy for advertisers targeting people 18 to 49 years of age with at least $50,000 in household income. It costs about $49 per thousand to reach this prime group on television but only about $12 on the Internet (Hafner & Tanaka, 1996; Warren, 1999).

Lower CPMs may actually translate into higher costs when advertisers pay for viewers that are not their target consumers. The price of reaching a select group may often be more expensive through television and newspapers than through the Web despite its higher CPM. CPM comparisons among the Web and other media should be undertaken with caution and other factors should be considered, especially the cost of reaching 1,000 targeted individuals against the cost of reaching just any 1,000 people in the mass audience (Boyce, 1998).

While making time and space purchases, media planners may consider audience quality a more important determinant than cost. In the long run, advertisers need to get their messages to the audience that is most receptive to their products and services and most likely to become first-time and repeat purchasers.

Traditional media CPMs are often based on circulation figures, the number of subscribers, or local market size and ratings, all of which are verifiable, reliable, and often audited figures. Lacking a reliable audience measurement system, the Web relies on gross estimates of the number of site visitors and the number of those who are actually exposed to an advertising message. Thus, Web CPMs are highly questionable, as are Web CPM comparisons among media. Eventually, flat-fee and CPM models may be replaced with more precise Web-based pricing measures. Until then, advertisers, agencies, and Web site operators are struggling with creative ways to effectively price Web spots (Edmonston, 1995; Schwartz, 1996).

The New York Times on the Web posts its Online Media Kit (http://www.nytimes.com/adinfo/rates.html). The media kit outlines the cost of running a Web ad, CPMs, guaranteed impressions, and maximum run times. The media kit page also provides information on audience demographics, Web site traffic, production specifications, and sales contracts (see Figure 3.6).

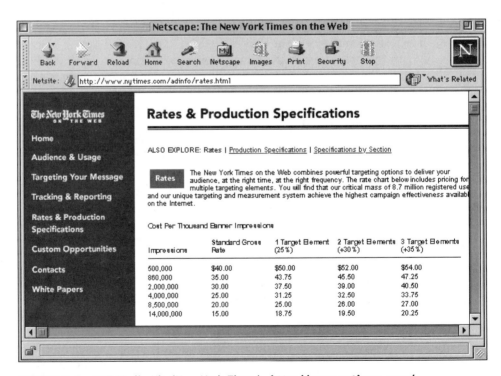

FIGURE 3.6 NYT Media Kit (New York Times), **http://www.nytimes.com/adinfo/rates.html**

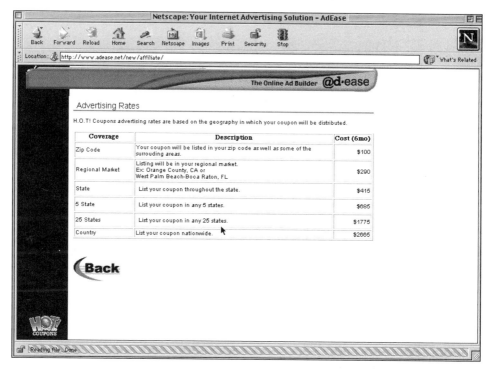

FIGURE 3.7   H.O.T! Coupons Ad Rates, **http://www.adease.net/new/affiliate/**

The cost of purchasing banner ad space depends on the number of visitors, the response rate, the size of the banner, and other considerations such as online ready or contract discounts. Posting a banner ad can cost tens of thousands of dollars depending on the site and number of impressions. But high costs should not scare advertisers away from the Web because there are plenty of popular sites that charge reasonable rates. H.O.T! Coupons (http://hotcoupons.com), a popular coupon site, sells local electronic coupon banners for as little as $100 for a 6-month posting (Advertising Rates, 1999), as Figure 3.7 shows.

The Web Digest for Marketers (http://www.wdfm.com/advertising), and Standard Rate and Data Service (SRDS) (http://www.srds.com/media_resource/index.html), a provider of media rates and data for the advertising industry, both post handy online CPM calculators. Simply plug in the cost of an ad and its reach, and the calculator figures out the CPM. It also calculates the cost when CPM and exposure are entered, and figures exposure when cost and CPM are known (see Figure 3.8).

Click-Through Rates

Banner ad **click-through rates** (**CTRs**) (or pay-per-view rates) are based on the percentage of Web site visitors who click-through a banner ad. The rates are calculated by dividing the number of users who click on an ad by the number of users

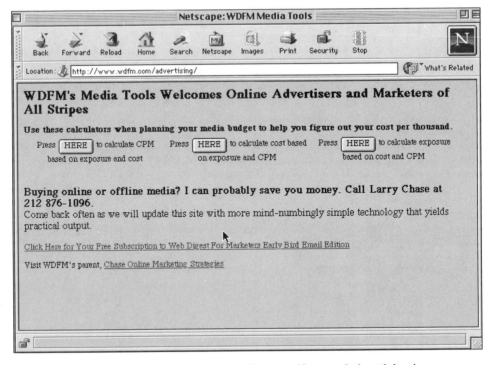

FIGURE 3.8   WDFM—CPM Calculator, **http://www.wdfm.com/advertising/**

who see the ad. For example, if 30 out of 1,000 people who see a banner ad actually click on it, the ad has a click rate of 3 percent. Advertisers are charged only for the 30 people who actually expressed an interest in the ad and not for the 970 people who landed on the site but did not click on the ad. The formula is simply

Number of click-throughs/Number of exposures

30 people click on an ad/1,000 people saw the banner = 3 percent

Click-through rates are more suitable for some types of online ventures than for others. For example, push services are in the business of sending content to customers. The number of visitors who come to their site may actually be lower than the number of people who receive their content through their push service. Therefore, push services would be shortchanging themselves by charging just for the number of visitors to their site. It makes more sense and can be more profitable for push services to charge for the number of pay-per-views regardless of whether users click-through from information that is pushed to them or from information that they pull from the site.

The advertising networks Aaddzz (http://www.aaddzz.com) and Value Click (http://valueclick.com/ad.html) are firm believers in click-through pricing.

Aaddzz charges advertisers $200 per 1,000 click-throughs (20 cents each) and also gives advertisers the choice of paying per impression instead of click-through, but believes that click-throughs are the better deal. Aaddzz tracks each banner ad and page against individual users and then in real time delivers a banner that has the highest chance for click-through (Bruner, 1997).

Procter & Gamble was one of the first companies to insist on paying only click-through rates for its Internet advertising. Since then, P&G has altered its stance and now supports a hybrid impressions and performance model but still curtails its online advertising because of a lack of effective ad pricing models (Voight, 1996; Williamson, 1999b).

In early 1999, P&G stunned the industry when it announced that it would pay a $5 cost per thousand rate for its banners. It has yet to be seen how many sites with space to sell will take P&G up on its offer, especially since it is far lower than the average $36 per thousand they typically receive (Maddox & Ross, 1999).

Advertisers hoping for crowds of customers clicking on their banners may be disappointed. Only between 1 to 13 of every 100 individuals who see an ad click on it. Anything over a 3 percent click-through is unusual. Advertisers are especially disappointed with the news that click-through rates are declining. In 1994, click-throughs hovered over 10 percent, but have been steadily decreasing ever since. It was observed that in the last half of 1998, click-through rates dropped by 50 percent (Vonder Haar, 1998b). More recently, most advertisers are lucky if they see a response rate as high as 2 percent. The decline is generally attributed to the explosive increase in banner ads and the fact that users no longer think of the ads as a novelty so their levels of curiosity have waned (Hutheesing, 1996; "Improving Their Swing," 1998; Voight, 1996; Warren, 1999).

In the early days banners were such a novelty on Web sites that surfers eagerly clicked around sites just to see what was going on. Now many surfers are no longer intrigued with banners. They have also found that banners do not deliver the excitement promised to them. Additionally, many surfers just do not have the time to bother clicking on an ad. People often access the Web for specific reasons (such as shopping, seeking information or research, or trying to connect with others) and they do not want to get sidetracked. Another reason that click-through rates have dropped is plain boredom. Banners just can not always deliver much that is new and exciting. Since more and more banners are appearing on Web sites because publishers are able to sell more space, there are more choices for the potential clickers to choose from ("Click-Through Rate Falls," 1999).

A study conducted by AdKnowledge (http://www.focalink.com/index.html) shows that online advertisers should reconsider the value of click-through rates. According to this study, click rates have little value as indicators for return on investment (ROI) optimization because their correlation to conversion rates is so low ("AdKnowledge Proves Click Rates Ineffective for Web Marketing Optimization," 1999).

An acceptable CTR may depend upon the product being advertised. If the economics of the process are considered, a sliding scale for CTR rates may make sense. If a banner that is selling a $5 item receives a low CTR, then very few dollars will be generated from the site. If the banner is selling a $2,000 item, the CTR can be much lower and still generate as many dollars in sales as a high CTR for a low-dollar-amount item. Therefore, the acceptable CTR should be tied to the desired or necessary sales volume that is supposed to be generated from the site.

Another consideration about CTRs is that the specific audience may also be very important. When the product is expensive golf clubs, a high number of click-throughs from people 12 to 17 years old is not valuable. Conversely, when the product is inline roller skates, a high click-through rate from people 65 and over is simply not helpful to the marketing effort.

Although click-throughs are generally decreasing, sometimes the rates can be inflated when a banner "tricks" the audience into clicking, only to have the audience completely reject the sites to which they are linked. Some banners make very strong promises such as "Win Millions," "Make Money at Home without Having to Work," "Lose Weight without Dieting or Exercise," "Best Rates for Air Travel," or other pie-in-the-sky come-ons when they simply cannot deliver on those promises. Virgin Airways learned the hard way that misleading ads are unacceptable in cyberspace. In 1995 the U.S. Department of Transportation fined the airline $14,000 for posting an ad that listed a low fare between Newark, New Jersey, and London that was not available. That was the first time the department charged an airline for misleading ads on the Internet ("Airline Fined," 1995).

A number of nonfunctioning representations are also used to trick the audience. Phony interactive features such as pulldown menus, keyword searches, scroll bars, and play buttons appear on a banner to let the user think that there is some actual utility or entertainment about to happen. Instead, when the user clicks on a button on the banner, the user is brought directly to an advertiser's site regardless of the user's intent. In other words, the graphics make the banner appear usefully interactive, when in fact the buttons or other graphic devices do nothing. After a few bad experiences with these, users become very suspicious. This suspicion translates into even lower click-through rates for banners that offer genuinely attractive utilities. In other words, trick banners may teach people to avoid banners with interactive content (Thompson, 1999).

Click-through rates often depend on where banner ads appear on the screen. In the early days of the Web, pages would download from top to bottom. Content at the top of the screen became visible before content at the bottom of the page. Advertisers used this downloading pattern to their advantage by placing banners at the top of the page. The banner would then be the first image consumers would see as the page appeared on the screen. Once **interlacing** technology became available, Web pages no longer download in an unrolling fashion, but instead the whole page comes into focus all at once (Waltner, 1996).

Interlacing works by first displaying a low-resolution version of the entire image or page, then the resolution increases in stages until the highest possible resolution is reached and the image or page is fully focused. With interlacing, the top of the page no longer holds as big an advantage for advertisers, and ads are now commonly placed at various locations on a page rather than dominating the top

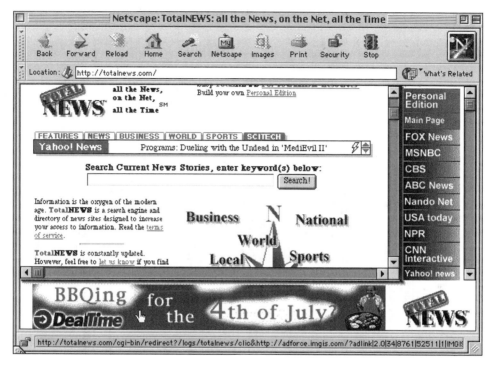

FIGURE 3.9   http://totalnews.com

spot. On some sites, such as TotalNEWS (http://totalnews.com) where content is framed, banners are located at the bottom of the screen (see Figure 3.9) and remain there as users scroll through the content (Holden & Webster, 1995).

Advertisers seek the page position where their banners will be most visible and will receive the most clicks. University of Michigan students researched the best location on a page for a banner ad. They found that banner ads placed next to the right scroll bar in the lower right-hand corner of the screen had a 228 percent higher click-through rate than banners placed at the top of the page. Additionally, banners inserted about one-third of the way down the page were clicked-through 77 percent more often than banners at the top of the page (Gupta, 1997). Apparently, the old way of thinking that the top of the page is the best location for a banner ad no longer holds true (see Figure 3.10).

Even though page location can improve click-through rates, the response rates still remain much lower than advertisers would like them to be. As an Internet Advertising Bureau spokesperson said, "One of the bedrock problems is a lack of trustable research. There's no bedrock yet in this medium, like in television, where there's 40 years of research to show what a 30-second spot can do" (Napoli, 1999).

FIGURE 3.10 Drugstore.com ad on the bottom right by scroll bar

Time Spent Listening/Viewing

Radio and television broadcasters often base advertising rates on the amount of time the average person spends listening or viewing during a particular hour or quarter-hour. With broadcast, a 60-second spot typically costs more than a 30-second spot on the same program. There has been some talk that online pricing should model itself after radio's **time spent listening** (**TSL**) or television's **time spent viewing** (**TSV**) rather than just on number of visitors. People who spend greater amounts of time reading a page and traveling within a site are more valuable to advertisers than those who just land on a page for a few seconds and then move on to another site. TV Guide Online (http://www.tvguide.com/tv/) boasts to potential advertisers that its users spend an average of 16 minutes on its site.

Adapting the TSL and TSV models to the Web would provide advertisers with the number of site visitors along with the amount of time they spend on a page. Advertisers could relate the amount of time visitors spend on a site to the likelihood of their clicking on a banner. Advertisers would then have a clearer idea of how much time they have to attract visitors to their banners. This broadcasting pricing model transfers to the Net with banner pricing schemes based on how long the ad stays on the screen. The Internet service company, AdCast (http://www.adcast.com) combines timed spot advertising with interactivity. Advertisers display their banners for a pre-set duration ranging from 15 seconds to a minute and a half. Advertisers put the time to good use by showing ads that "tell a story" similar to television commercials. "Instead of impressions, advertisers get minutes" (Vonder Haar, 1999a, p. 31). On AdCast partner sites, banners are displayed in a box in the lower left-hand corner of the screen and remain there while viewers scroll or click around the site. Counting on an average visit of 5 minutes in length, AdCast delivers between 8 and 10 timed messages per viewing session.

Size-Based Pricing

Borrowing from conventional newspapers' advertising pricing structure, the cost of a banner ad is sometimes based on the amount of screen space it occupies. Newspapers charge for display ads according to the paper's circulation and the size of the ad. Charges for newspaper ads are assessed according to a specific dollar amount per standard column inch area, whereas banners rates are measured by pixel area. **Size-based pricing** is calculated by multiplying an ad's width by its height in pixels. After the number of square pixels is calculated, a fee is assessed per pixel or by the total area (Snyder & Rosenbaum, 1996).

Size-based pricing has not caught on in the cyberworld. Very few Web sites use this method of pricing alone. Instead many sites use a variation of size-based pricing along with either CPM or click-through measures. A site may charge a different flat fee, CPM, or click-price for a smaller banner than for a larger one.

Cost per Transaction

Cost per transaction (CPT) is another way to charge for online ads, but with this method the price is based on response or sales. Advertisers are assessed a minimal charge or, in some cases, no charge at all for ad placement; actual costs are based on the number of consumers reached (Schwartz, 1996). As one Internet analyst put it, "An impression that doesn't convert someone is a lost impression" (Mand, 1998).

CPT is similar to per-inquiry (PI) fees charged for broadcast advertising where stations negotiate a fee or a percentage of the advertiser's net or gross sales based on the number of inquiries that can be directly attributed to the ad. Metropolitan Life Insurance Company wrapped up a year-long campaign on MSN Sidewalk (http://national.sidewalk.msn.com), which tested new software that tracked MetLife prospects from the time they click on an ad until the day they sign on with MetLife (Williamson, 1999a).

CPT deals, especially those that combine some sort of low flat rate with a transaction commission, have emerged as another way to bring revenue to a Web site besides merely selling ad space. Online merchants are weary of investing advertising dollars that may not lead directly to sales, and high-traffic Web sites are eager to earn a commission on top of a small fee for delivering an audience.

Barnes & Noble (http://www.barnesandnoble.com) cut itself a good deal with MSNBC (http://www.msnbc.com) and CNN. Barnes & Noble promotes its book titles by placing banners next to news stories on the same topics. For example, when CNN ran a story about the shootings at a Kentucky high school, it placed a link next to the story for books about teenage violence. CNN and MSNBC collect a commission for each book sold from the links and Barnes & Noble benefits from increased sales (Hansell, 1997).

Other content providers are less than thrilled with the idea of result-based fees. Although they feel it is their responsibility to deliver an audience to their advertisers, they do not feel that they should take responsibility for a poor sales record. An ill-designed ad or high product price can each be enough to deter consumers from ordering a product. Complicated ordering procedures, poor return policies, and slow servers are also barriers to completing transactions. These and other obstacles are out of the Web site provider's control, so they feel that they should not be penalized with low advertising revenue just because an advertiser cannot sell its product—the risk is on the Web site provider and not the advertiser.

CPT models may not be for everyone. Not all marketers are set up for electronic selling. Some marketers that advertise on the Internet to increase brand awareness may not be set up to conduct online transactions; here CPT models are of no use. Also, simply keeping track of sales can be a nightmare. Online sales data are elusive for providers whose systems are not set up to automatically track these types of records. Until its partnership with MSN Sidewalk, which tracks sales generated by banners, MetLife had no way of knowing whether someone who saw a banner ad ended up buying insurance. Gaining favor are pared-down versions of CPT models that base advertising fees on the number of visitors who request more information or fill out online forms and other data sheets that are easier to track than sales (Mand, 1998).

Hybrid Deals

Some advertisers feel that they are not getting the best possible deal by paying for straight impressions or just for clicks, and others would like to throw cost-per-transactions into the pricing mix. Advertisers are calling for **hybrid pricing** structures to maximize their return on their Internet advertising investment. Speaking in support of hybrid pricing models, the chairman of the Internet Advertising Bureau asserts, "The hybrid model is for e-commerce advertisers who are looking to generate sales as a result of banner advertisements and links. This is really equitable for both parties because the media site gets valuation for its audience. The advertisers get a [model] that's more performance based. In this case, both parties get what they want" (Mand, 1998, p. 48).

In reality, hybrid rates consisting of a flat-rate payment along with some combination of transaction revenue sharing, click-throughs, or cost per sale accounted for 52 to 56 percent of ad deals in 1998. Straight cost per thousand and **sponsorships** accounted for another 40 to 43 percent and the remaining were strictly based on click-throughs or other performance-based rates (Maddox, 1998b; Maddox, 1999).

Selecting a Pricing Structure

Advertisers and Web site operators prefer the pricing structure that best matches their needs. Unfortunately, how advertisers think their costs should be assessed and how Web site managers think they should be charged are often very different. No one pricing mechanism is preferred by all online advertisers. Direct marketers tend to prefer paying click-through fees, whereas advertisers more interested in building brand awareness go for CPMs. Forrester Research found that out of 52 major Web advertisers, slightly more than one-quarter favor click-through rates, slightly less than one-fourth like result-based fees, 15 percent prefer CPM rates, and the remaining one-third prefer some sort of a hybrid or combination pricing formula (Forrester Research, 1996).

ALTERNATIVE ADVERTISING BUYS

Online advertising can be a risky venture, especially for smaller businesses with thin wallets that are hesitant to spend their advertising dollars on a new and un-proven medium. Advertisers only need to do a bit of searching to find advertising exchanges, co-op deals, discounts, and auctions through which they can join the top advertisers without stretching their finances. Many sites and services offer dis-counted rates for unsold spots. Advertisers benefit from low fees and Web space providers benefit by filling spots that would otherwise go unsold.

Ad Auctions

More Web sites mean more ad space, and more ad space means more advertise-ments are needed to fill the slots. Some estimates claim that as much as 50 to 70 percent of spots on the top 500 Web sites go unsold (Berst, 1998). Smart entrepre-neurs have stepped in to help broker the unclaimed space at reduced rates. **Ad auctions** are thriving as Web site providers agree to sell at a low price, and ad-vertisers are jumping all over discounted space.

San Francisco–based OneMediaPlace (http://www.onemediaplace.com), (see Figure 3.11) grew from a company that sold excess ad space for Web sites at dis-count prices to a company that is a meeting place for media buyers and sellers. Originating with the idea that getting discounted rates for unsold space is better than not getting any money at all, the company now provides an array of services based on unsold inventory in online, outdoor, and broadcast media.

Ad auctions in general seem to be more popular with second-tiered sites that put themselves above auctions. Publishers that may not have a large sales force or may not be well known have the opportunity to show advertisers that their sites can deliver an audience. And advertisers are more willing to take their chances on less popular sites and perhaps a new medium if they are paying a discounted price (Flynn, 1998; Walmsley, 1999).

Just because they are buying auctioned space does not mean that advertisers are stuck with whatever sites come their way. Adauction gives buyers several

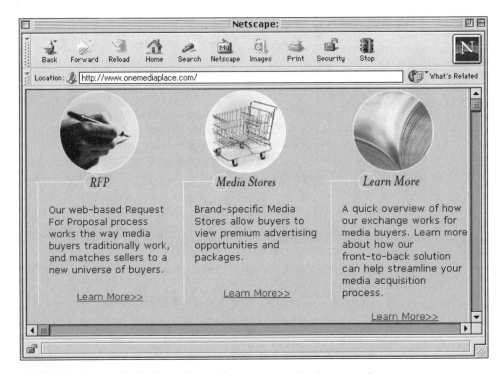

FIGURE 3.11   OneMediaPlace, **http://www.onemediaplace.com/**

purchasing options. Buyers choose bargain space from category-specific areas, such as finance and women's interests; they also can select from among different ad pricing models and opportunities such as sponsorships and e-mail. Adauction and other auction sites are trying to shed the image of being places to get good deals on leftover ad space. They would like to be known as locations where advertisers can "get valuable inventory that can be bought quickly, cheaply and to scale" (Riedman, 1998).

Advertising Exchanges

Although many smaller businesses have terrific Web sites, they can not afford aggressive online campaigns. One way to get the word out is through **advertising exchanges** where advertisers place banners on each other's Web sites for free. MSN Link Exchange/bCentral (http://www.adnetwork.bcentral.com) (Figure 3.12) works on a quid pro quo basis where advertisers help direct traffic to each other's sites. Member companies exchange free advertising space on their Web site for a free spot for their own banner on another company's site (Resnick, 1997).

SmartClicks (http://www.smartage.com/smartclicks/index.html) is another free banner exchange program especially for small and midsize businesses. For

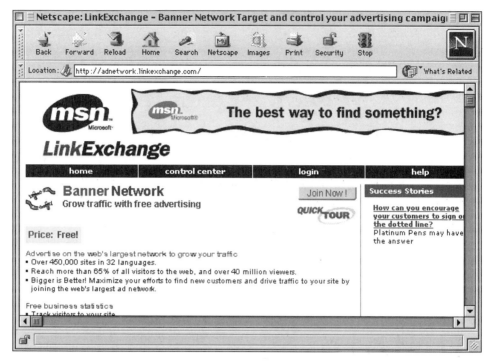

FIGURE 3.12   MSN Link Exchange/bCentral, **http://adnetwork.bcentral.com/**

every two impressions Web site providers post on their site, they get one banner credit to advertise their product on someone else's site.

Advertising exchanges are gaining in popularity, especially among marketers with shallow pockets and those without large sales teams. By trading space, advertisers experience new sites that they may not have been able to afford and they may find new outlets that reach their target audiences.

Cooperative Advertising

Calling it **cooperative advertising,** Amazon.com (http://amazon.com) and other booksellers have recently started charging book publishers to promote titles on their sites. Amazon.com's staff typically reviews books and writes short descriptions along with recommendations, whereas cooperative advertising allows publishers to do their own promoting. At first, Amazon.com did not point out to customers that certain recommendations were being paid for by publishers. After receiving sharp criticism, the company now posts a page that explains its publisher-supported placement policy and lets users knows which ads are part of the co-op program.

Amazon.com is both a bookseller and a respected book reviewer, and some book lovers are concerned that its co-op program will blur the lines between the site's content and advertising content. Amazon.com promises to be true to its customers and holds that most of its editorial areas are not for sale. What is for sale, however, is its "What We're Reading" area, which charges publishers $500 to list a title for two to three days. Other premium packages can cost up to $10,000 for home page displays and promotions (Carvajal, 1999).

Box 3.1 ■ AMAZON CO-OP PLACEMENTS

One of the ways Amazon.com categorizes its books is by topic. A book lover can select an area of interest and see its hot new titles without having foreknowledge of a book's existence. At the bottom left of the topic page—in this example, Mystery and Thrillers—is a link called Supported Placements on this Page (see Figure 3.13).

Clicking on the "Supported Placements" link brings up a page that explains Amazon's co-op placement program and lists publisher-supported books of the week (see Figure 3.14). In this example, clicking on *Middle of Nowhere: A Novel* link brings up a shopping page showing the featured book's cover and price plus book reviews (see Figure 3.15). If a user traveled to the shopping page via the route described, he or she would be aware that the book *Middle of Nowhere: A Novel* is a product placement. However, users can take several other routes to the shopping page, such as by entering a key word search or by following other links on the Mystery and Thrillers page. These users would have no way of knowing that the book is a co-op placement because there is no indication of such on the shopping page.

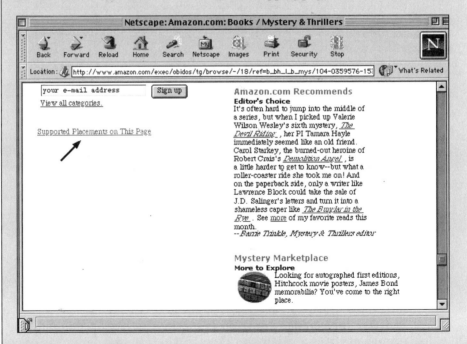

FIGURE 3.13   Amazon Co-op Link, **http://www.amazon.com/exec/obidos/tg/ browse/-/18/ref=/b_bh_l_b_mys/104-0359576-1536735**

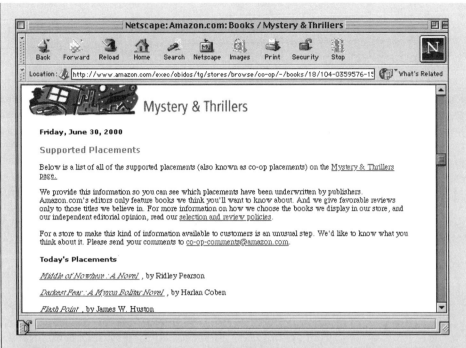

FIGURE 3.14 Amazon Co-op Page 2, **http://www.amazon.com/exec/obidos/tg/ stores/browse/co-op/-/books/18/104-0359576-1536735**

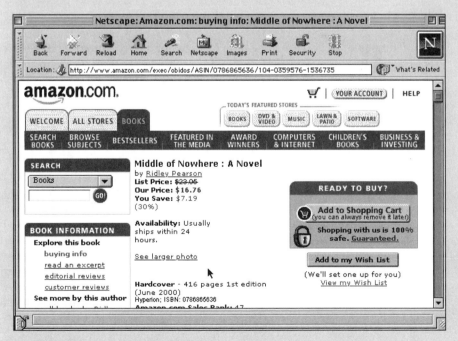

FIGURE 3.15 Amazon Co-op, **http://www.amazon.com/exec/obidos/ASIN/ 0786865636/104-0359576-1536735**

Discounts

Most traditional print publications offer advertisers camera-ready discounts for advertisements that are complete and ready for page paste-up. Some Web sites offer similar discounted rates if banners come in "online-ready," meaning fully coded in HTML and complete with all graphic, audio, or video files. Additionally, sliding fees can be formulated based on how much formatting the Web site manager has to do to an ad before posting it online.

Advertising inventory is not always quickly snatched up, leaving many Web site operators with unsold spaces. Shrewd advertisers know how to bargain for these open slots. Rather than paying full price, advertisers negotiate for a **minimum bid price,** (the lowest rate the seller will accept) or for a **blind buy** (discounted space sold off at the last minute, sometimes for as low as 20 percent of the full rate) (Berst, 1997).

AdOutlet (http://www.adoutlet.com) sells ad space from a storefront site that looks and feels like any other online retail site. The enterprise positions itself as an online marketplace for buying and selling advertising space. The site offers last-minute ad space at fixed costs up to 80 percent off the full selling price. Different from other purveyors of excess ad space, AdOutlet does not auction the inventory but sells it at set discounted prices (Vonder Haar, 1999b).

SUMMARY

There is little doubt that online advertising is becoming a mainstay of marketers and advertisers and that they now face the task of adapting to the new environment. The emergence of online advertising has fostered a new kind of advertising and new types of advertisements, and has necessitated modifying broadcast and print pricing models and initiating new cost structures.

Changes in the online world are coming fast with advertisers and marketers leading the way. Ever since the Web browser Mosaic hit the market, online commercialism has thrived and has made many inroads into the online world.

Simple, nonanimated banners were the first to hit the online scene. But advertisers needed to answer the public's call for more visual and audio excitement. Rich-media ads in the form of interstitials and superstitials began sprouting up in the corners of computer screens. Ads were no longer just sitting there but were now flashing and flying in front of users' eyes and treating them to lively video and audio. Stimulation-hungry viewers still begged for more so webmercials were born. Now, watching a computer screen is just like watching a television screen where full-motion video commercials drone on for up to 30 or so seconds. On one hand, the hard-to-satisfy public craves visually stimulating ads, but on the other hand, they scream at the intrusiveness of cybercommercials.

While users are adapting to the crazy world of online advertising, advertisers and Web site providers are grappling with issues of their own. How much ads should cost and how much advertisers should pay is a never-ending debate. Which pricing model is best—CPM, click-throughs, sized-based, cost per transaction, or some combination thereof—is the question that the advertising industry is asking. Many advertisers are shunning posted ad rates and instead are buying through a process of bidding. With so much leftover ad space, there is little reason to pay full cost and space providers figure it is better to sell space at a discount than to not sell the space at all. Better yet, there is little reason to pay for space when it is just as easy to exchange a banner for a spot.

All these and many other issues loom as advertisers, marketers, and the Internet population sort out what online advertising is and what it should become. In the meantime, commercialism lives and grows in the frontier called *cyberspace.*

Discussion Questions

1. Why do you think people are more likely to click on rich-media ads or v-banners than text-only banners?
2. Why do you think people have negative attitudes toward infomercials/advertorials on the Internet? Do you think advertisers should be required to distinguish their sales pitches from product information? Why or why not?
3. What kinds of products and services are best suited for each of the different types of ads mentioned in this chapter?
4. From a consumer perspective, what are the advantages and disadvantages of the different types of online advertising?
5. From an advertiser's perspective, what are the advantages and disadvantages of the different types of online advertising?
6. If you were a marketer with space to sell on your Web site, which advertising pricing method or combination of methods would you use?
7. If you were an advertiser, which pricing method would most appeal to you?
8. What are the advantages and disadvantages of co-op advertising to Web site providers, advertisers, and consumers?
9. Why do you think banner ads are being clicked on with less frequency than before?
10. Why do you think ads placed next to the scroll bar on the right side of the page generate a higher click-through rate than ads placed at the top of the page? What other page locations do you think would be as effective?

Chapter Activities

1. Emarketer predicts that by 2001 only about one-quarter of all online ads will be in the form of the banners of today. New technologies will allow the production of new forms of online advertising. Design a cyberad that has not yet been created. Use your imagination.
2. Find several plain banners and rich-media ads that promote similar products, services, or ideas. Compare the plain banners to the rich-media banners. Which ads do you find most attractive and which would you be most likely to click on? Why?
3. Click on several banner ads. What happens after you click? Do pop-up windows appear, are you whisked off to an advertiser's home page, or do order forms magically appear? Track the number of clicks it takes to get to product information and order forms.
4. Imagine that you are the advertising manager for a small, local business. Determine your target market and select several Web sites on which to post your banners.

Determine the cost of ad placement and your target audience reach. Which Web site is the best value for your advertising dollars?

5. Find several examples of trick banners. Identify the strategies that trick the audience.

References

AdKnowledge proves click rate ineffective for Web marketing optimization. (1999, August 16). *Focalink.com* [Online]. Available: http://www.focalink.com/corporate/press/pr_990913_click_rates.html

Advertising rates. (1999). *H.O.T. Coupons Web site* [Online]. Available: http://www.adease.net/new/affiliate/ (1999, October 11).

Airline fined for misleading ad. (1995, November 22). *St. Louis Post Dispatch,* p. 7A.

Austen, I. (1999). But first, another word from our sponsor. *The New York Times on the Web* [Online]. Available: http://www.nytimes.com/search (1999, June 22).

Berst, J. (1997, November 10). What you don't know about Web ads will cost you: Jesse Berst's Anchor Desk. *ZDNet.com* [Online]. Available: http://www.zdnet.com/anchordesk (1998, December 4).

Berst, J. (1998, June 16). Web advertising woes: Jesse Berst's Anchor Desk. *ZDNet.com* [Online]. Available: http://www.zdnet.com/anchordesk (1998, December 4).

Bovee, C. L., & Arens, W. F. (1986). *Contemporary advertising.* Homewood, IL: Irwin.

Boyce, R. (1998, February 2). Exploding the Web CPM myth. *Advertising Age* supplement, *Online Media Strategies of Advertising,* p. A16.

Bruner, R. E. (1997, September 8). Small networks chase per-click ad business. *Advertising Age,* p. 38.

Carvajal, D. (1999, February 8). For sale: Amazon.com's recommendations to readers. *The New York Times on the Web* [Online]. Available: http://www.nytimes.com/search (1999, February 19).

Cleland, K. (1996, September 4). Web narrows gap between ads, editorial. *Advertising Age,* pp. S3, S14.

Click-through rate falls. (1999, September 27). *Emarketer* [Online]. Available: http://www.emarketer.com/enews/122198_lan.html

Easton, J. (1996, December). Hidden revenue hotspots. *ZD Internet Magazine,* pp. 99–106.

Edmonston, J. (1995, August). When is a Web ad simply too costly? *Business Marketing,* p. 18.

Flynn, L. J. (1999, March 4). Battling perceptions, auction firms hope to sell leftover online as space. *New York Times on the Web* [Online]. Available: http://www.nytimes.com (1999, February 19).

Folb, M. (1999, December 13). What is a superstitial and why would I use it? *Marketing Magazine* [Online]. Available: http://www.unicast.com/about/index_news.html (2000, February 5).

Forrester Research, Inc. (1996). *Media & technology strategies* [Online]. Available: http://www.forrester.com (1998, January 21).

Gupta, S. (1997). Banner ad location effectiveness study. *WebReference* [Online]. Available: http://Webreference.com/dev/banners (1998, February 1).

Hafner, K., & Tanaka, J. (1996, April 1). This Web's for you. *Newsweek,* pp. 74–75.

Hansell, S. (1997, December 8). Links between news and ads raise concerns in new media *The New York Times on the Web* [Online]. Available: http://www.nytimes.com/search (1999, February 19).

Head, S. W., Sterling, C. H., & Schofield, L. B. (1994). *Broadcasting in America.* Boston: Houghton Mifflin.

Holden, G., & Webster, T. (1995). *Mastering Netscape 2.0.* Indianapolis: Hayden Books.

Hutheesing, N. (1996, May 20). An online gamble. *Forbes,* p. 288.

Improving their swing. (1998, February 2). *Advertising Age* supplement, *Online Media Strategies for Advertising,* p. A45.

The Internet Index. (1997, October 10). *Open Market homepage* [Online]. Available: http://www.openmarket.com/intindex

Johnson, B. (1998, November 2). ZDNet's new "extramercial" puts entire screen to work. *Advertising Age, 69* (44), p. 42.

Maddox, K. (1998a, September 21). Ad networks test rich media across sites. *Advertising Age, 69* (38), p. 36.

Maddox, K. (1998b, November 2). IAB: Ad revenue online projected to hit $2 bil in '98. *Advertising Age, 69* (44), p. 38.

Maddox, K. (1999, February 15). IAB: Internet advertising will near $2 bil for 1998. *Advertising Age, 70* (7), p. 34.

Maddox, K., & Ross, C. (1999, January 18). P&G pushes Web as sellers to swallow low-ball rates. *Advertising Age, 70* (3), pp. 1, 46.

Mand, A. (1998, March 30). Beyond hits & clicks. *MediaWeek, 8* (13), pp. 48, 52.

McCloskey, B. (2000, January 27). The forms of rich media: Part I. *ClickZ Network* [Online]. Available: http://www.unicast.com/about/index_news.html (2000, February 5).

Mendels, P. (1997, September 29). Dilemma for kids Web sites: Separating fun stuff from ads. *New York Times Online* [Online]. Available: http://www.nytimes.com (1999, February 19).

Millward Brown Interactive report finds superstitials more effective, more positively perceived than other online formats (1999, October 25). *PR Newswire* [Online]. Available: http://biz.yahoo.com/prnews/991025/ny_superst_1.html (2000, February 5).

Napoli, L. (1999, June 17). Banner ads are under the gun—and on the move. *The New York Times on the Web* [Online]. Available: http://nytimes.com/search (1999, June 22).

Rebello, K., Armstrong, L., & Cortese, A. (1996, September 23). Making money on the Net. *Business Week,* p. 104.

Resnick, R. (1997, February). Marketing riddle. *Internet World* [Online]. Available: http://pubs.iworld.com

Richtel, M. (1997, April 19). TV-type ads emerge on the Web. *The New York Times on the Web* [Online]. Available: http://nytimes.com/search (1999, February 19).

Riedman, P. (1998, September 28). Adauction moving to daily sale of online ads with Tune-In. *Advertising Age, 69* (39), p. 48.

Schwartz, E. I. (1996, February). Advertising Webonomics 101. *Wired,* pp. 74–79.

Snyder, H., & Rosenbaum, H. (1996). *Advertising on the World Wide Web: Issues and policies for not-for-profit organizations.* Proceedings of the American Association for Information Science, 33, pp. 186–191.

Tedeschi, B. (1998, October 7). Study finds ad banners make an impression. *The New York Times on the Web* [Online]. Available: http://nytimes.com/search (1999, February 19).

Tedeschi, B. (1999, January 26). Ads that are too rich for publishers' pipelines. *The New York Times on the Web* [Online]. Available: http://nytimes.com/search (1999, June 22).

Tedesco, R. (1999, November 8). Web ads get glitzy, savvy. *Broadcasting & Cable, 129* (46), p. 49.

Thompson, D. R., & Wassmuth, B. (1999). *Do they need a "trick" to make us click? A pilot study that examines a new technique used to boost click-through.* A paper presented at the meeting of the Association for Education in Journalism and Mass Communication, New Orleans, LA.

Voight, J. (1996, December). Beyond the banner. *Wired,* p. 196.

Vonder Haar S. (1999a, May 17). AdCast sells time-based ads. *Interactive Week,* 6 (20), p. 31.

Vonder Haar S. (1999b, June 14). Web retailing goes Madison Avenue route. *Interactive Week,* 6 (24), p. 18.

Walmsley, D. (1999, March 29). Online ad auctions offer sites more than bargains. *Advertising Age, 70* (13) p. 43.

Waltner, C. (1996, March 4). Going beyond the banner with Web Ads. *Advertising Age, 67,* p. 22.

Warren, C. (1999, Fall). Tools of the trade. *Critical Mass,* p. 22.

Web clutter, etc. (1999, September 1). *Kiplinger's Personal Finance Magazine, 53* (9), p. 28.

Wingfield, N. (1997, February 11). It was inevitable: Webomercials. *C/Net homepage* [Online]. Available: http://www.news.com/News/Item/0,4,7821,4000.html

Williamson, D. A. (1999a, January 18). MetLife backs local agents with sidewalk sponsorship. *Advertising Age, 70* (3), p. 38.

Williamson, D. A. (1999b, May 3). Web still hunts big-grand spenders. *Advertising Age, 70* (19), pp. s8, s20.

Chapter 4

Online Advertising Opportunities

ONLINE PLACES TO ADVERTISE
 Web Sites
 Portals
 Local/Regional Sites
 Chatrooms
 Online Games
 Classified Sections
 E-Mail
 Newsletters
 Intranets
ONLINE PROMOTIONS
 Coupons
 Sweepstakes
 Sponsorships
 Product Placement

Little thought was given to banners when they first appeared in 1994 on HotWired's Web site. Few advertising executives imagined that the Web would become the hottest advertising medium around or that they would be adding the Web to the advertising mix. Advertising executives typically faced annual media plans that included only a few budget line items. Print ads or broadcast commercials received the majority of funding, typically 70 percent or more. Approximately 15 percent of the ad budget was allocated for direct mail, with 7 percent for public relations and the remainder for miscellaneous expenses. By the 1990s media planning and budgeting were dictated by new line items, such as place-based and in-home media, interactive direct mail, infomercials, electronic public relations, and online services. Rather than shifting resources from the traditional media advertising budget, a separate line item has been established for the Web. Companies are finding that Web sites and other new media initiatives that increase interaction between customers and companies are well worth their budget allocation (Cross, 1994; Napoli, 1996).

Although some advertisers may hesitate to jump online, others are not shy at all and the Internet community happily welcomes them. There are many advertising opportunities on the Internet including placing banners in Web sites, portals, online games, and chatrooms. There are also opportunities for local/regional buys, classifieds, coupons, sweepstakes, newsletters, e-mail, sponsorships, and advertorials. Advertisers have the job of wading through all of the available spots and choosing the ones that best deliver the audience they are seeking for a price they can afford.

This chapter takes a look at some of the more popular places to advertise on the Internet and then identifies several different types of online promotions: sponsorships, product placement, sweepstakes, and coupons. These promotions have been singled out because they can appear in many locations throughout the Internet and are not confined to one particular location, such as classifieds appearing on classified pages. Coupons may be an exception, as they appear both on special coupon sites as well as throughout the Web.

ONLINE PLACES TO ADVERTISE

There are plenty of places on the Internet in which to post promotional messages. When most people think of Web advertising, they think of banner ads on Web sites. But some Web sites have become more specialized and able to attract targeted audiences and subgroups of users. Portals, local/regional sites, chatrooms, games, and classifieds are all excellent advertising opportunities. For something different, some advertisers are sending commercial messages through e-mail, newsletters, and intranets.

Web Sites

Advertisers can choose from among tens of thousands of Web sites on which to place their advertisements. There is a site out there for everyone. Advertisers need to spend their money well. Whether on the Internet or in traditional media, they have to buy the most bang for their buck. Advertisers can not afford to waste any money by advertising on sites just because they are there and just because they want to be online.

Advertisers have a wealth of online targeting opportunities. By advertising on sites that draw their targeted audience, advertisers can amass thousands of new customers. Web sites can be categorized by the products and services they offer, and each attracts visitors with unique demographic characteristics. Automotive sites, computer sites, online pharmacies, online television and entertainment networks, cyber travel centers, and so on reach audiences that are easily targeted by advertisers.

While many advertisers choose Web sites that will deliver an audience likely to purchase their products, Shell International has taken a different approach by placing banner ads on sites whose audiences are likely to be hostile toward its products.

Shell International banners have appeared on such sites as activist magazine Mother Jones (http://www.motherjones.com), Environmental News Network (http://www.enn.com), and The Economist (http://www.economist.com). The banners link readers to pages on Shell's Web site that explain its position on such issues as human rights and the environment. Shell's objective is to educate and initiate dialog with skeptics and to position itself as being socially responsible (Guilford, 1999).

Portals

More than just a Web site, a **portal** is a multipurpose megasite that combines news, entertainment, information, searching, e-mail, chat, and other services all in one location. Portals offer a one-stop shop for consumers to use as an alternative to surfing from one site to the next. By having something for everyone, visitors may drop by for one service, but then discover another and then another, and then get hooked and become portal loyalists.

Portals may attempt to hold on to their customers and encourage repeat visits by registering their entrants. Registered users tend to have a greater sense of commitment to the portal and are more likely to become repeat visitors than are other people. Registered users of Yahoo! (http://www.yahoo.com) and Netscape (http://www.netscape.com) clocked in four times as many page views as nonregistered users during April 1999. For Yahoo! this meant an average of 238 page views per registered user compared with 58 page views per freewheeling surfer (Vonder Haar, 1999d).

Many advertisers are turned on by portals because they draw repeat visitors and large numbers of people with many different interests and needs to the same location. "If you can stuff enough services and content into a single Web address, you will, in the ugly parlance of the industry, 'aggregate eyeballs' . . . so that the owners of the portal can sell advertising priced on a certain dollar amount for every 1,000 pages viewed" (Fixmer, 1998).

Box 4.1 ■ TOP NINE PORTALS OF 1997

The top nine portals of 1997 snagged 59 percent of all Internet advertising.

1. Alta Vista (http://www.altavista.com)
2. America Online (http://www.aol.com)
3. Excite (http://www.excite.com)
4. Infoseek (http://infoseek.go.com)
5. Lycos (http://www.lycos.com)
6. MSN (http://www.msn.com)
7. Netscape (http://www.netscape.com)
8. Yahoo! (http://www.yahoo.com)
9. Snap (http://www.snap.com)

Ironically, many portals once functioned solely as search engines that directed visitors to other Web sites, but now they are the desired destination.

The portal concept has taken a new direction by mixing transactions with content and community. For example, Warner Bros. Online (http://www.warner-bros.com) has taken on marketing partners, which, for between $25,000 and $50,000, get placement within its portal for 6 weeks. For the 1998 Christmas season, Warner Bros. Online fashioned a Holiday Shopping Picks area with links to online retailers such as Levi-Strauss, Dockers, iVillage, and 3Com. Advertisers on Holiday Shopping Picks were more than happy with click-through rates that averaged 11.5 percent (Maddox, 1999).

Community-oriented portals, also known as affinity portals, strive to reach groups of people by ethnicity, age, or sexual orientation. These portals serve the specific purpose of providing an all-in-one community for these groups. Black Voices (http://blackvoices.com) serves as an affinity portal for the African American community. Asian Avenue (http://www.AsianAvenue.com) caters to Asian Americans, and there are several portals for Hispanics, including LatinoLink (http://www.latinolink.com). Several sites with banner ads in the Chinese language, including SineNet (http://home.sina.com/index.html) and Chinese Cyber City (ccchome.com), are aimed at Chinese Americans.

The gay population, college students, and the elderly among others are the targets of many portals. Planet Out (http://www.planetout.com) is an alternative to gay-oriented print publications. Almost one-third of gay people polled responded that they did not have access to gay-oriented publications because their local stores did not stock such magazines and newspapers or they felt too uncomfortable purchasing the publications in public. Planet Out gives gay people a sense of community, and advertisers have a select market at a low cost. The CPM for a full-page ad in Planet Out's print counterpart, *Out Magazine,* costs about $127 compared to $18 to reach 1,000 visitors to the Planet Out Web site (Farrell, 1999). Planet Out even urges visitors to shop from its gay-friendly advertisers.

Student Advantage Network (http://www.studentadvantage.com) and CollegeClub.com (http://www.collegeclub.com) are just two of many affinity portals reaching out to that elusive university crowd. Advertisers such as AT&T, Amtrak, MCI, Textbooks.com, Staples, Tower Records, and Vitamin World fill the screens of these college-oriented portals that offer students advice about such issues as dealing with stress, financial aid, and college life in general. These portals are also connected to the cultural scene. They provide movie, book, and music reviews, follow the hottest rock band tours, and give students tips on the latest fashions.

The biggest hurdle facing portals is that, to consumers, many of them look and operate alike. Many of the better known portals, especially those that were once known as search services, are indistinguishable from their competitors. The visual designs are similar and they provide the same features and services. A test of portal identification found when six leading portals' logos were erased from the screen, only 2 out of 100 Internet users could correctly name the portals. Without their logos, these portals have few if any distinguishing components. When users can not tell the difference between portals, they do not develop loyalty to one particular portal. This lack of loyalty diminishes the portal's ability to deliver a steady audience to its advertisers. According to Jupiter Communications, only about 5 percent of advertisers say they are likely to renew their agreements with portals unless they can demonstrate they can build loyalty and repeat business and can develop a strong brand image (Siegel & Zolli, 1999).

Local/Regional Sites

Regional ad placement services are springing up to provide advertisers with area-wide Web advertising coverage. Advertising sales collectives make it easy for companies and services to reach local consumers with one advertising buy rather than negotiating with each online publisher individually. For example, the representatives for New York Regional Advertising Program (NYRAP) (http://www.nyrap.com) may sell space on all member sites. NYRAP agents may sell space for the online versions of Long Island–based *Newsday*, the *Village Voice*, several Gannett-owned regional newspapers, local radio stations, and other regional/local media. Advertisers can cover the New York/New Jersey/Connecticut region or any local tri-state area with one buy from NYRAP (Outing, 1997).

MSN Sidewalk (http://national.sidewalk.msn.com) is an arts-and-entertainment guide to about 75 cities across the United States with links to Yellow Pages, retailers, and other businesses. When first-time visitors select a city, a menu page appears with links to local happenings and promotions. MSN Sidewalk has signed on more than 6,000 local advertisers such as car dealers, retailers, restaurants, and realty companies that pay as little as $100 dollars a month (Johnson, 1998).

The benefits of regional services are summed up by a Saatchi & Saatchi executive who claims that about 80 percent of all business transactions take place within 20 miles of a consumer's home (Hodges, 1996). Local advertising in the form of classifieds, local business sites, and customizable ads by ZIP code accounted for nearly 12 percent of total online ad revenues in 1997 (Hyland, 1998). Further, according to the Kelsey Group, by 1999 the local business market favored the Web as the third most popular advertising medium behind Yellow Pages and newspapers. Figure 4.1 shows the Netscape local ad program page.

Chatrooms

Online chatting is one of Internet users' favorite pastimes so advertisers are tapping into the power of talk by taking their promotions inside chatrooms. While some marketers may be hesitant to try advertising in chat venues, most are enticed by the overwhelming number of online gabbers. Many chatrooms and discussion forums are topic-centered and thus attract audiences with common interests, hobbies, and lifestyles, driving advertisers to vie for the opportunity to reach these targeted audiences. Chatrooms are becoming such a popular venue for posting product messages that by the end of the year 2000 they are expected to contribute close to $1 billion of the total online advertising revenue (Cleland, 1996).

America Online started placing ads in its chatrooms after realizing that more than 70 percent of its users were chatters and that they were logging more than one million hours of chat every day. AOL chat sessions with celebrities draw tens

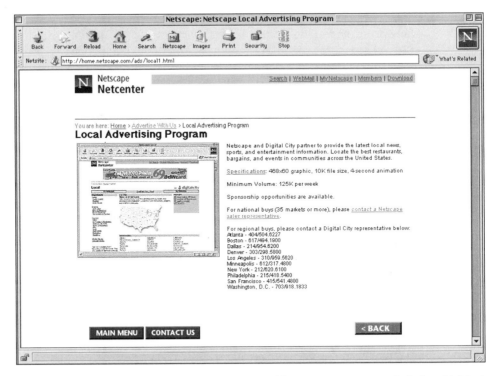

FIGURE 4.1　Netscape Local Ad Program, **http://home.netscape.com/ads/local1.html**

of thousands of participants simultaneously—an audience that is hard for advertisers to ignore (Auchard, 1999).

　　Talk City (http://www.talkcity.com/chatpages/enter.htmpl) bills itself as an online community that supports discussions, chats, and other entertainment fare. The site has partnered with NBC, Cox Cable, and others who "raise their profile with mainstream advertisers" (Riedman, 1998b p. 40). The site brings in close to half of its revenue through advertising from such heavy hitters as Amazon.com and VISA.

Online Games

Web sites that feature games attract young, loyal, imaginative players who are a prime audience for many products, especially those directed toward males. Most players of online games are men between the ages of 18 and 34 who stay on for 25 minutes to more than one hour (McGinty, 1997).

　　Several search services that have expanded into portals are now offering game areas. Excite, Yahoo!, Lycos, and Infoseek have all added so-called **sticky products** in the form of games designed to keep users at the site for long periods of time

(Katz, 1999). Lycos's gaming area keeps visitors there for about 28 minutes on average, four times longer than on the rest of the site. But length of time on a site does not guarantee that players will click on the banners they see. Many are afraid that if they do click on a banner, they will lose their place in the game or somehow cancel the game before its completion. The gaming site Uproar occasionally reminds players to click on the banners and reassures them that their games will not be lost if they stop to respond to an ad (Riedman, 1998a).

You Don't Know Jack (http://www.won.net/channels/bezerk) is a popular site for advertisers that like their ads popping onto the screen after every five or six questions. The ads are with-it and attention getting. An important part of the game, they raise the overall feeling of fun and excitement.

Rather than running traditional banners, some companies are sponsoring games and contests on gaming sites. Tower Records and Tower Movies sponsor music and movie trivia games on Uproar (http://www.uproar.com). For example, one game is listed as an active link for Tower Rock/Pop Trivia (Figure 4.2).

In an effort to increase response, Sony Online Entertainment (http://www.spe.sony.com) offers its advertisers more pay-per-play opportunities on its Wheel of Fortune (http://www.spe.sony.com/tv/shows/wheel) and Jeopardy (http://www.spe.sony.com/tv/shows/jeopardy) game areas. Wheel of Fortune players

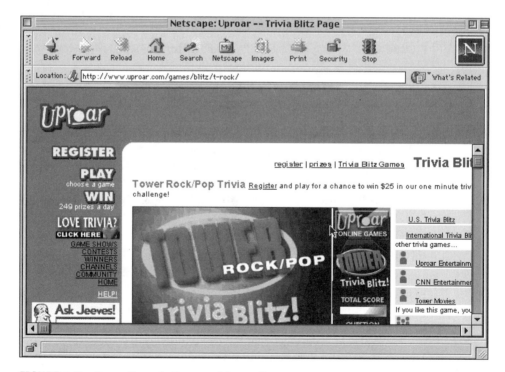

FIGURE 4.2 Tower Records Sponsorship on Uproar.com,
http://www.uproar.com/games/blitz/t-rock/

get an extra spin or a free vowel if they click on the displayed banners; Jeopardy is also selling ad space on new incentive buttons. These new advertising models are in addition to the traditional rotating banners that are visible at the top of the screen even as players are guessing Jeopardy clues or selecting letters on Wheel of Fortune.

To increase response rates, some companies are using other creative strategies such as making clicking-through a fun activity by linking users to interactive games and contests. Interactive Imaginations' Riddler (http://www.riddler.com) packs its site with a variety of games, puzzles, scavenger hunts, crossword puzzles, contests, and other amusements. The site requires players to click on banner ads to participate in any of the activities. Targeted consumers are lured to advertisements through their desire to play games or enter contests. In exchange for personal information such as age, occupation, and media use, users can play for cash awards, cars, Caribbean cruises, and other fantastic prizes. In its first two years online, Riddler awarded its players over $300,000 in cash and prizes (Resnick, 1997).

Using banner ads as a gateway to its site has proven to be an effective and profitable strategy for Riddler (Figure 4.3). Players have fun and sometimes win prizes, advertisers create awareness for their products and gather marketing information about their audience, and Riddler profits from a wildly popular site that

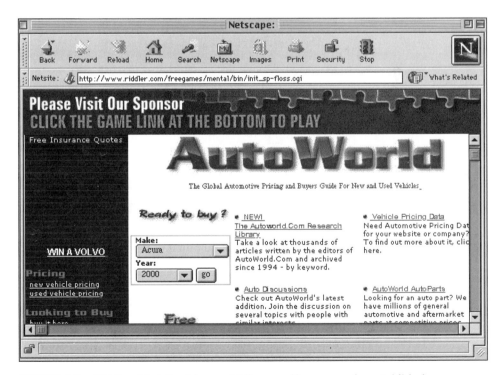

FIGURE 4.3   Riddler Ad, **http://www.riddler.com/freegames/mental/bin/ init_sp-floss.cgi**

brings in revenues from charging advertisers for every individual who clicks-through (Hutheesing, 1996).

Classified Sections

Whether searching for jobs across the country, looking for a summer home in another state, seeking a classic car, or just being curious about what people are selling, online classifieds are the place to go. As one newspaper spokesperson remarked, "The Internet is probably the most significant new event we've had since someone figured out what a classified ad is" (Kelly, 1996, p. S23).

Classified ads account for almost 40 percent of newspapers' overall revenue, translating into about $40 billion annually. Classifieds are the most profitable type of advertising newspapers carry. Newspapers are now hoping to reap a profit from posting their classifieds online. Classified ads have long been a strong revenue-generating service for newspapers and a favorite section with readers. And now, newspapers are taking their classifieds online to boost their revenues and to promote themselves globally (Kelly, 1996; Napoli, 1999).

Global promotion is not limited to U.S. newspapers. Many newspapers from around the world are promoting themselves on the Web and are competing for the global audience. For example, a majority of readers of online publications from India actually live outside of the country. Therefore the publications' banner and classified ads are targeted both toward Indians living in India and toward those living overseas (Pashupati & Raman, 1999).

Offering print and Web advertising as a one-price package increases classified revenues and balances the ratio of print to online ads. Additionally, newspapers are nudging their classified advertisers to the online world. USA.net (http://usa.net) is working with newspapers to set up free temporary e-mail boxes for all print-based classified advertisers. This way advertisers can receive responses without having to give out personal information such as telephone numbers or addresses (Vonder Haar, 1999a).

Industry experts predict that 60 percent of all online newspapers will soon offer a classified section. The newspapers that do post classifieds online have seen their revenues steadily increase from 1996—when classifieds were only a $100 million business—with expected growth between $1.5 and $1.9 billion by the year 2002 (Kelly, 1996; Napoli, 1999).

Newspapers face losing almost 10 percent of their printed classifieds to sites such as employment services and others that specialize in classifieds. Instead of running a classified in the *San Francisco Chronicle* employment section, for example, a personnel director may opt to place the ad on a specialty career Web site that can draw prospective employees from around the globe rather than just from the San Francisco Bay area. To offset these losses, newspapers need to generate additional revenue by competing head-to-head with specialty classified sites (Fessler & Shinkle, 1997; Vadlamudi, 1997).

Further erosion of classified revenues comes from the inclusion of URLs in print display and classified ads. Newspapers are concerned that businesses will place their URLs within their ads to direct readers to their Web sites (where they will try to sell them their goods and services) rather than purchasing a larger ad to do the selling. At one time, the *Patriot News* in Harrisburg, Pennsylvania, barred a realty company from including its URL in its classified ads. Some newspapers charge premiums for URLs printed in ads, while others would not even think of prohibiting them and even make them into clickable links when posted online. As one publisher said, "Could we imagine telling people they could not publish their address or phone number in their advertisement?" (Outing, 1998).

Although the competition may be fierce, newspapers are banking on their brand name and their sales ability to hold their own against specialty classified sites. *The New York Times* and *Chicago Tribune* post their employment, auto, and real estate classifieds free of charge to their Web site customers. The *Chicago Tribune* initially charged advertisers a small fee to post their ads on the Web, but has since restructured its classified system so that advertisers are now charged for both print and Web classifieds as part of a package deal (Kelly, 1996). Figure 4.4 shows a Chicago Tribune employment ad.

Newspapers generally offer their classifieds on their home sites, but some are combining their efforts and listing their classifieds en masse on neutral Web sites. Several online ventures compile classified listings from newspapers around the

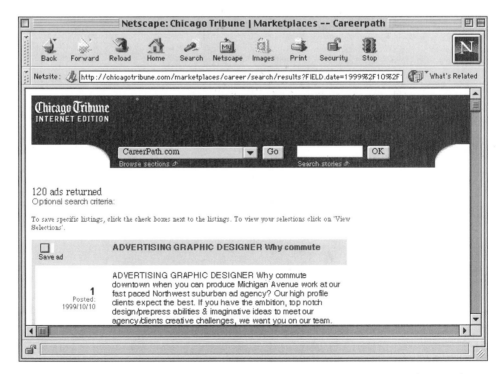

FIGURE 4.4   Chicago Tribune Employment Ad. When *advertising* Is Entered as a Job Search Term on the Chicago Tribune Employment Classifieds, 120 Job Listings Are Returned. **http://chicagotribune.com/marketplaces/career/search/**

country into searchable databases. New Jersey Online (http://www.nj.com) offers classifieds from three regional state papers, and CareerPath (http://careerpath.com) combines employment classifieds from over 57 newspapers nationwide. CitySearch (http://www.citysearch.com) provides real estate classifieds for major U.S. cities as well as acting as a regional entertainment and information guide.

Two classified sites represent hundreds of newspapers across the country. Classified Ventures (http://www.classifiedventures.com) was founded by seven leading media companies, and PowerAdz (http://www.poweradz.com) has newspapers as investors, but is not controlled by newspapers. The merged newspapers' classifieds have one highly visible site on which to place their ads. PowerAdz's AdQuest3D posts more than 350,000 classifieds daily from 1,400 newspapers in their network. These consortiums provide the technology that individual newspapers do not have for turning print ads into searchable databases. According to the vice president of the Newspaper Association of America, classified consortiums arose from the need for newspapers to compete with nontraditional sources. "We want to direct consumers to newspaper advertising online because consumers see those classifieds as real ads. They have an innate feeling of certain reliabilities you can ascribe to newspaper advertising" (Napoli, 1999).

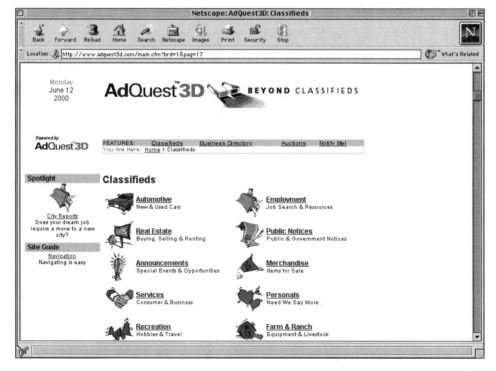

FIGURE 4.5   PowerAdz, **http://www.poweradz.com**

E-Mail

As the most widely used Internet resource, e-mail has caught the eye of advertisers. With banner ad click-throughs remaining very low and viewers becoming so accustomed to banners that they no longer notice them, marketers are sending their promotions out via e-mail. Database marketers, such as 24/7 Media (http://www.247media.com), create e-mail campaigns for their clients and then send out promotions to a highly targeted list of consumers. A&E Television Network promoted its *Live by Request* program via ConsumerNet, which sent audio-enhanced e-mail to target prospects. A&E's vice president of marketing asserts that e-mail advertising is "a better, more concise, less expensive way to get to people one-on-one" (Lorge, 1999). It is also "incredibly difficult to send unique messages to unique people, simultaneously and in volume" and "even relatively simple e-mail marketing efforts can devour resources" (Shachtman, 1998, p. 38).

Well-known companies such as Hotmail (http://www.hotmail.msn.com), Juno Online (http://www.juno.com), and NetCreations (http://www.netcreations.com) have initiated advertiser-sponsored e-mail services (Figure 4.6). These and similar enterprises are betting that their users will tolerate and even welcome

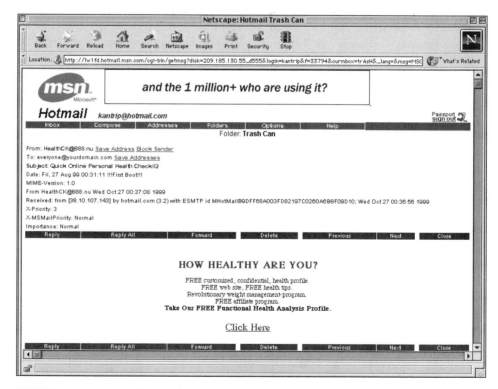

FIGURE 4.6 A Hotmail E-mail Ad for Health Analysis in a Message,
http://lw1fd.hotmail.msn.com

advertising messages creeping onto their screens in exchange for free e-mail access. Users receive ads either as banners as they open their mailboxes or as e-mail messages.

Microsoft-owned Hotmail might well be the hottest free electronic mail service available. Although Hotmail subscribers get e-mail services free of charge, they "pay" by accepting personalized news feeds and advertisements. By spring 1998, Hotmail claimed 13 million subscribers and was signing up 80,000 new registrants per day. Hotmail's 7 to 10 million unique monthly visitors frequently push it into monthly rankings of the top 25 most visited Web sites. Subscribers are drawn to Hotmail's hassle-free system that is accessible from any computer or browser. Added perks include a built-in spell-checker, a thesaurus, and other writing tools for e-mail perfectionists. Hotmail is reluctant to reveal its actual revenues, but estimates claim that money brought in from advertisements is increasing between 15 to 20 percent each month (Gajilan, 1998; "Hurricanes and Football," 1999; "The Top Twenty-Five," 1997).

Juno Online is an Internet multiservice company that requires its 7.2 million subscribers to download a special software package available on the company's Web site. Subscribers do not have to have Internet access to retrieve their messages but can pick up their messages by dialing a local access telephone number. Juno offers three levels of service. Subscribers can opt for full Internet access through Juno Web, enhanced e-mail that can send and receive attachments through Juno Gold, and basic free e-mail. But with all this free access come advertisements. Juno subscribers are delivered rotating banners and interstitials that interrupt a subscriber's session and require subscriber interaction.

According to its Web site, NetCreations is a provider of "opt-in e-mail marketing services" that help "publishers, cataloguers, and other direct marketers reach prospects quickly and cost-effectively." The company's resource, PostMaster Direct Response, acts as a list manager and broker for more "than 3.5 million unique e-mail addresses in more than 3,000 topical categories." NetCreations is careful to ask its subscribers what types of promotions they would like to receive. Someone interested in computers could sign up to receive special offers for software and hardware. Advertisers that sign on with NetCreations have their ads transmitted to targeted consumers for as little as 10 to 15 cents per e-mail, a huge savings over mailing rates charged by the U.S. Postal Service.

New to the Internet scene, Topica (http://www.topica.com) promises an easy way to subscribe to more than 40,000 topic-specific e-mailing lists. Billing itself as a central bank for creating and subscribing to lists, Topica operates under the premise that consumers are more receptive to e-mail promotions if they give their permission first and if they know they are giving permission rather than doing so unknowingly through sweepstakes or other interactions. Sensitive to its users' privacy, Topica believes that permission is only one part of the process—the other is to deliver promotions in a nonthreatening manner (Vonder Haar, 1999b).

Promotions by e-mail become even more intense as improved technology stuffs in-boxes with video and audio sales messages that contain direct links to more product information. Start-up Mind Arrow (http://mindarrow.com) envisions sending prospective customers data-intensive video files that can be as large as 400,000 bits. By linking these e-mails to a central server, advertisers can monitor the number of times a user plays the video e-mail or clicks for more information. Prospective clients who demonstrate interest through interaction can then be targeted for additional information and follow-up sales calls (Vonder Haar, 1999c).

E-mail may appear to be a promising method of delivering commercial messages, but it has captured the wrath of users who are up in arms at receiving unsolicited sales pitches. While many companies take care not to clog e-mail systems with unwanted solicitations, others are not as conscientious. Many e-mail address holders resent receiving advertisements through what is considered to be a personal electronic mailbox. After being bombarded with excessive and unwanted promotions, the public has come to think of e-mail advertising as unacceptable and often refers to it by the unflattering term **spam**. According to Web folklore, there are two origins of the word *spam*. Some say the term comes from the popular Monty Python saying, "spam, spam, spam," which was nothing more than a meaningless uttering, although pronounced with an English accent, of course. Other claims that e-mail spam is akin to the canned sandwich filler—a whole lot of junk but no real "meat."

Spam is officially known as "anything unsolicited, anything that is out of context, or out of the customer's expectations for amount, frequency, or content, or anything that requires you to opt-out of something you've never chosen in the first place" (Tedeschi, 1998b). The line between spam and legitimate e-mail is blurred when marketers send information that customers signed up for—even if they did so unwittingly.

From a marketer's standpoint, sending out promotional material via e-mail is much more efficient than waiting for potential customers to stumble upon their Web page or one of their banner ads. It only takes a few seconds for users to recognize and delete an unwanted promotional message, so marketers figure that recipients are spared any real harm—but this kind of thinking can backfire on the advertisers. Unsolicited e-mail can be detrimental to advertisers because customers who are spammed could harbor negative feelings and may boycott the company's products and services. According to *Internet Week* magazine, it costs tens of millions of dollars—about $2 per user—each month in customer service time, bandwidth, and systems administration time to delete junk e-mail. Additionally, a Gartner Group Inc. survey showed that 84 percent of e-mail users have been assaulted with spam, and half of them open or delete junk e-mail an average of six times per week.

While many people blast spamming, others feel that old-fashioned **netiquette** (polite Net behavior) should acquiesce to free enterprise. One such defender of spamming is Sanford Wallace, also known as the Spam King. Wallace is president of Cyber Promotions Inc., a bulk e-mail company that makes its server available to its clients to send unsolicited e-mail. For a small fee, anyone can deluge the network with junk e-mail and they can even disguise or "spamouflage" their return addresses so they can not be identified (Miller, 1999). Cyber Promotions has been the target of several lawsuits. The company's opponents claim that if every business were allowed to jam up the network with unsolicited e-mail, the whole system could shut down. Efforts are under way to make spamming illegal, and several companies have developed software that blocks junk e-mail, though none are 100 percent fool-proof (Branscum, 1997).

After much pressure, even the King of Spam himself has vowed to help clean up junk mail. Although he believes he has a constitutional right to send ads by e-mail, he has promised the Federal Trade Commission that he will help stop abusers (Miller, 1999).

Organizations such as the *Coalition against Unsolicited Commercial E-mail* (CAUCE) (http://www.cauce.org) and spam.abuse.net (http://spam.abuse.net/) are fighting for legislation that will protect the online community from unwanted e-mail. ChooseYourMail heads up the Spam Recycling Center (http://www. chooseyourmail.com/spamindex.cfm), where consumers can forward their spam e-mails. The center then forwards the messages to the Federal Trade Commission. In a two-month period in 1999, the center collected almost 200,000 pieces of junk e-mail (Freeman, 1999).

Public outcry and legal actions are serving their purpose, as only about 10 percent of legitimate businesses continue to send out unwanted e-mail ads. With almost 9 out of 10 marketers appropriately using the Web and the enactment of new guidelines, e-mail advertising just may emerge as an acceptable delivery system for many types of commercial messages.

Newsletters

Subscription-based newsletters are gaining in popularity as an advertising venue. Just as people subscribe to their favorite magazines that get mailed to their home addresses, many are subscribing to **e-mail newsletters** and information sheets that are transmitted to them on a regular basis. E-mail newsletters are hot advertising vehicles because they deliver a targeted audience that is already interested in products relating to the newsletter's content. These **opt-in e-mail** pieces are delivered directly to current and potential customers who have subscribed to the list.

Opt-in e-mail is basically a way for marketers to deliver their news electronically rather than through the U.S. mail. It is more cost efficient to electronically deliver information than to send subscribers a printed version through the post office. According to E-target.com (http://www.e-target.com), an opt-in e-mail marketing service, the first-year start-up costs for direct e-mail marketing, including mailing lists and server costs, is between $30,000 and $36,000. However, the start-up and mailing costs—including paper, envelopes, printing, and stamps—for sending the same number of customers a printed version would run about $257,000. Clearly, there is a great financial incentive to electronically transmit newsletters rather than to mail them out in the more conventional fashion ("Comparison," 1999).

Within opt-in e-mails marketers promote new products, provide updates on existing products, and communicate with their customers about the company in general. The newsletters themselves are promotional so some companies choose to confine their online advertising efforts to this outlet and they may not accept advertising from other sources. Procter & Gamble's Neighbor to Neighbor offers parenting advice along with product news about its laundry soap Tide, and each week Lands' End sends about 200,000 subscribers its newsletter full of company and product information (Zbar, 1999).

Other newsletters are topic specific, rather than company promotional, and these may accept advertisements. TipWorld (http://www.topica.com/tipworld) is an online publisher of computer-related information on such topics as the Internet and software. It delivers over 3.5 million newsletters to subscribers in 170 countries around the globe. TipWorld delivers an interested and loyal audience for a CPM of about $30. Advertisers get a half-screen banner ad and several text-only mentions scattered throughout the newsletter so readers are bound to see the ad (Resnick, 1997).

Intranets

Web site operators are not the only ones profiting from selling online ad space. Companies are getting in on the action by selling ads on their own intranets. An **intranet** is a company's own network of computers. Intranets are used for transmitting proprietary and open information to employees throughout the corporation. The initial costs of establishing an intranet can be high and selling ads is a good way to offset the expenditures. Product logos and sales messages like "Nike, Just Do it" crawl across the tops of employees' computer screens as they check their e-mail.

Even schools are giving in to commercialism. Cash-strapped and technology-desperate schools are entering into partnerships with firms such as ZapMe!, Highwired.net, and ScreenAd that donate free computers and Internet services in return for allowing ads on the classroom screens. The ZapMe! browser embeds rotating ads on the lower left-hand corner of the screen, and Highwired.net creates free Web sites for student newspapers in exchange for packaging ads within the pages. ScreenAd installs screen savers with rotating banners on computers and splits the ad revenue 60:40 with the schools (Forber, 1999).

Classrooms have traditionally been commercial-free. Even in the late 1980s a big fuss was made when schools wanted to accept free televisions in exchange for showing Whittle Communication's Channel One, which aired ads within the newscasts. Although some parents and educators are troubled by these ads-for-equipment deals, they are becoming increasingly common as schools struggle with the expense of wiring classrooms (Stone, 1998).

ONLINE PROMOTIONS

Advertisers are experimenting with new ways to capture online consumers. In the offline world, coupons, sweepstakes, sponsorships, and product placement are effective means of advertising. Coupons and sweepstakes bring an immediate response to the advertiser and benefit the consumer with discounts or prizes. Sponsorships and product placement are more subtle ways of promoting products. They do not directly scream "Advertisement!" at consumers, but they do build brand awareness. Advertisers are taking these traditionally offline promotions and successfully adapting them to an online environment.

Coupons

Web shoppers are no different from anyone else in their desire to find a bargain, and **coupons** are the ticket to many good deals (see Figure 4.7). The Web is alive with the sight of coupons. Store coupons, product coupons, and service coupons are ripe for printing off the many coupon sites. H.O.T! Coupons (http://www.hot-coupons.com) was one of the earlier ventures to establish a Web site where shoppers print coupons for local, regional, and national products and services (Figure 4.8). One of the best features is that users find local coupons simply by entering their home or work ZIP code or city. Users can then print the coupons and take them to their local retailers for discounts.

Some coupon outlets only serve local or regional markets. Coupon Café (http://www.couponcafe.net) posts coupons from only Northern Virginia and the Washington, D.C., area. A quick search for food coupons in the Chicago area

FIGURE 4.7   coolsavings.com Banner Ad on the Weather Channel Site, **http://www.weather.com/weather/us/zips/31602.html**

FIGURE 4.8   H.O.T! Coupons Home Page, **http://www.hotcoupons.com/**

yielded discounts from over eighty outlets, plus grocery coupons and deals with national chains, such as Fingerhut and Omaha Steaks.

H.O.T! Coupons and Coupon Café are not alone in the online world. Val-Pak Direct Marketing Systems (http://www.valpak.com), CouponPages (http://www.couponpages.com), and eSmarts (http://www.esmarts.com/coupons.html) are just a few of the thousands of coupon sites. Entering the search term *coupon* in Alta Vista yielded 756,060 listings—whether these are all bona fide coupon sites is debatable, but if even one percent of them are legitimate, that still leaves about 7,560 coupon sites. Clipping online coupons is easier and more fruitful than rifling through the pages of a Sunday newspaper or a weekly shopper. Many coupon sites neatly categorize their discounters under main headings such as automotive, entertainment, and restaurants. On some sites, coupons are further sorted for quicker online searching. Figure 4.9 shows a coupon on Val-Pak's site.

In the past, advertisers have been slow to post online coupons, but many are now including couponing as part of their Internet advertising campaigns. The best news for advertisers is the coupon click-through rate, which averages as high as 20 percent compared to a measly 2 or so percent for conventional banners. Advertisers have also found that online couponing is an excellent way to track response— they can find out whether "Person A saw my coupon ad on Web site A, went to my site, downloaded the coupon, and redeemed it at the store" (Tedeschi, 1998c).

FIGURE 4.9   Val-Pak Pizza Coupon, **http://www.valpak.com/select/ret_coupon_ spec.shtml?$COUPON_ID=2668191&$ADDRESS_ID=25170966** (Entered ZIP Code 60646, Selected Restaurants, and Clicked on a Restaurant's Name)

Advertisers have found ways to expand their marketing efforts by offering their coupon clippers additional incentives and discounts in exchange for personal information including shopping habits. Based on that information, advertisers can tailor their coupons to specific types of customers.

Cybercouponing is just at least as advantageous as print coupons. Localized cybercoupons attract new customers who live nearby and who are thus especially likely to become repeat shoppers. Further, consumers can print out-of-area coupons that they can take with them on vacation. From 1996 to 1997, online coupon redemption soared by 500 percent, and it does not appear to be slowing down (Tedeschi, 1998c).

Despite recent coupon success stories, some consumers and businesses are hesitant to use such strategies. The potential for fraud fuels the resistance. Unscrupulous merchants or consumers can copy a coupon into a graphics program and then increase the coupon's face value. To minimize these practices the Association of Coupon Professionals (http://www.couponpros.com) tracks online coupon revenues and keeps on the lookout for fraudulent practices.

Sweepstakes

Sweepstakes is a new advertising strategy that is hooking those who love to take a chance. According to the Internet research company NetRatings, online sweepstakes is the fastest growing segment of online advertising. Sweepstakes banners represent almost 10 percent of all ads. Many well-known companies, such as Schick, Mars, Inc., and MasterCard, are jumping at the chance to learn more about their customers because, of course, entries are accompanied by demographic and other personal and identifying information.

Sweepstakes work for advertisers because they get the benefit of customers who have invested time in filling out the sweepstakes forms, and if customers know they have a chance of winning a prize they tend to give more accurate information. Just as important are the click-through rates. The top three banner ads tracked by NetRatings in July 1998 were all sweepstakes offers. In the same month, a banner for the U.S. Lottery generated an astonishing 48.6 percent click rate (Tedeschi, 1998a).

A variation of sweepstakes is the scratch-and-win banner. Rather than rubbing a coin against a playing card, prizes are revealed when users scratch off a ticket by moving their mouse back and forth across the electronic image. The marketing firm RealTime Media developed the scratch-off Java program and now plans to syndicate the technology to clients that can purchase online game cards in batches as small as 50,000. Individual marketers can tailor the game cards to suit their promotion and their branding needs. Lycos hit the jackpot with its scratch-and-win Superbowl promotion that brought in 88,000 registrations for personalized services (Vonder Haar, 1999e) (see Figure 4.10).

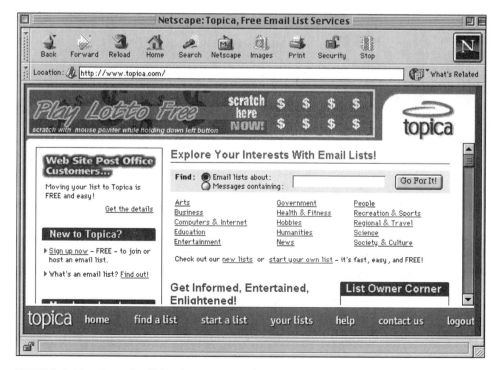

FIGURE 4.10 Scratch-off/Topica, **www.topica.com**

Many users do not view online sweepstakes as very credible, but as they start hearing about winners they may change their opinions. Online surfers have won Sony laptops, trips to New York, vacations in Rome, new homes, and hundreds of thousands of dollars all for only the click of a button and the price of personal information (see Figure 4.11 and 4.12).

Sponsorships

Cyber **sponsorships** also entice advertisers and bring in revenue. Online sponsorships are similar to television in the 1950s where one company would sponsor an entire program, such as Texaco sponsoring *Texaco Star Theater*. In cyberworld, instead of television programs, Web sites, chatrooms, and discussion forums are ripe for advertising sponsorships, which give companies exclusive rights to send their messages to a targeted audience.

Instead of selling banner ad spots, Web sites offer to share their online space with an advertiser/sponsor. Sponsorships are usually tied in with Web site content. Drug marketers are sponsorship-happy and will spend about $130 million online

FIGURE 4.11   Schick Sweepstakes: Banner of Schick Diamond Sweepstakes on MSN.com, **http://www.msn.com/**

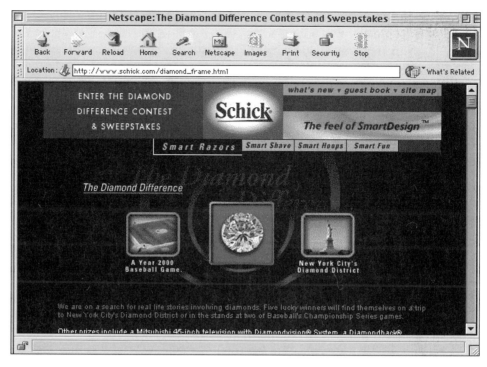

FIGURE 4.12   Clicked Schick Ad: Schick Sweepstakes Page after Clicking on Banner,
http://www.schick.com/diamond_frame.html

by 2002. The industry puts about half of its online investment into sponsorships, compared with about 30 percent for advertisers in general. With health information searches making up almost 40 percent of all online searches, the drug industry has a built-in market of consumers interested in their products (Neff, 1999).

When Claritin sponsored the Mayo Health Clinic (http://www.mayohealth. org/index.htm) and other medical sites in 1998, the Claritin site received more than 200,000 visitors per month with 90 percent of them clicking through from sponsorships or banners on other sites. While other drug companies may not experience the same successes as Claritin, they continue to move toward online sponsorships (Neff, 1999). For example, The Allergy Report, sponsored by Allernet allergy specialists, is one of CNN's better known sponsorships.

CNN Interactive also offers sponsorship packages in its Technology, Style, and Health sections, for special features such as CNNfn.com's Special Reports, and certain sports sections. Epicurious (http://www.epicurious.com), Condé Nast's gourmet-food cybersite, offers visitors a combination of editorial and advertising content with sponsor Robert Mondavi offering tips on serving the right kinds of wine with food.

Some sites are coming under fire for not clearly identifying their sponsors. Circuit Breaker was a happening San Francisco entertainment site in the mid-1990s until viewers caught on that the site was sponsored by Brown and Williamson Tobacco (maker of Lucky Strike cigarettes), which was not clearly indicated on the site. Before gaining access to interactive features, unsuspecting visitors were asked to share information about themselves, including whether they were smokers.

After users objected to the unidentified sponsorship, the Center for Media Education threatened to expose the site to the Federal Trade Commission for unethical business practices. Circuit Breaker added Brown and Williamson's logo to the home page and made it clear that the site was sponsored by the cigarette maker (Chapman, 1997). By the summer of 1998, Web users could no longer access the site without first typing in a password and user ID. More recently, the site could no longer be found.

Product Placement

When an adorable ET munched on Reese's Pieces in the movie *ET,* it sealed **product placement** as a viable alternative to traditional advertising. Product placement occurs when an advertiser's product is used or is visible within a movie or television program. A television or movie character drinking a Pepsi is an example of product placement, which can be just as effective as a traditional ad.

Product placement is not a new phenomenon. Even in the early radio soap opera *Oxydol's Own Ma Perkins,* references to the laundry detergent were often written into the script. Product placement has become more common in the past several decades and now products are being placed within Web "programs." In 1996, Honda and K Swiss were among the first companies to pay the now defunct online soap opera The Spot about $15,000 to weave a month's worth of product mentions into the story (Grumann, 1996).

SUMMARY

Online advertising has come a long way since the first text-only banners appeared on HotWired. Advertisers have discovered that placing banners on Web sites is not the only way to reach their customers. Portals, game sites, local/regional sites, intranets, and chatrooms often offer better opportunities for reaching customers. Additionally, newsletters, e-mail, sponsorships, advertorials/infomercials, and product placement give advertisers new ways to get their messages to the online public.

As the Internet expands and as new technologies develop, new ways to send out promotional material will surely emerge. As long as the Internet continues to offer advertisers efficient and economical ways to reach their audiences, online advertising is sure to continue its current boom and it will help establish the Internet as the medium of the new millennium.

Discussion Questions

1. What are the advantages and disadvantages of placing banner ads on Web sites that attract audiences that may be hostile to an advertiser's products, services, or ideas?
2. Why do you think affinity portals are so popular?
3. What types of products and services do you think would be most effectively advertised on each of the different types of online locations mentioned in this chapter?
4. If you were a newspaper publisher, would you allow your advertisers to put their URLs in their ads, especially if you knew that doing so allows them to buy smaller ad space?
5. Do you approve of e-mail advertising? What about spamming? Explain your opinion.

Chapter Activities

1. Visit an affinity portal. Who are some of the advertisers? Give examples of the ways the advertised products and services are targeted to the portal's audience. How do the portal's services attract its target audience?
2. Enter a chatroom that contains advertisements. Ask the chatters what they think of the ads. Keep track of their responses.
3. Play an online game that is sponsored by an advertiser. What did you learn about the advertiser from playing the game? Did the game draw you to the advertiser or did the advertiser draw you to the game? Did the advertising interfere with the game or with your enjoyment?

References

Auchard, E. (1999, February 19). AOL plans ads in chat rooms. *The New York Times on the Web* [Online]. Available: http://www.nytimes.com/search (1999, February 19).

Bannan, K. (1997, February 4). Peppery ads flavor the Web. *PC Magazine*, p. 29.

Branscum, D. (1997, May 12). King of "spam" and proud of it. *Newsweek*, p. 90.

Chapman, F. S. (1997, August). Web of deceit. *PC World*, pp. 145–152.

Cleland, K. (1996, August 5). Chat gives marketers something to talk about. *Advertising Age*, p. 22.

Cleland, K. (1998, November 16). Narrow-marketing efforts winning the Internet savvy. *Advertising Age, 69* (46), pp. s26–s27.

Comparison, (1999, December 2). *E-target.com* [Online]. Available: http://www.e-target.com/compare

Cross, R. (1994, October). Will new technologies change the marketing rules? *Direct Marketing*, pp. 14–40.

Farber, P. J. (1999, October 25). Schools for sale. *Advertising Age, 70* (44), p. 22.

Farrell, G. (1999, August 6). Web opens hard-to-reach markets. *USA Today*, p. 12B.

Fessler, K., & Shinkle, K. (1997, November 2). Papers go online to keep classified ad business. *The Stuart News*, p. D6.

Fitzgerald, K. (1996, March 18). A redeeming opportunity for local coupon providers. *Advertising Age*, p. 26.

Fixmer, R. (1998, July 27). From search engines to portal sites. *New York Times on the Web* [Online]. Available: http://www.nytimes.com (1999, February 19).

Freeman, L. (1999, September 27). E-mail industry battle cry: Ban the spam. *Advertising Age, 70* (40), p. 70.

Gajilan, A. T. (1998, April 13). You've got mail—and it's free. *Newsweek,* pp. 80–81.

Giles, M. (1998, October 18). Fighting spammers frustrating for now. *Atlanta Journal-Constitution,* pp. H1, H4.

Godin, S. (1999, May). Permission marketing: The way to make advertising work again. *Direct Marketing, 62* (1), pp. 40–43.

Grumann, C. (1996, February 21). Soap operas invade the Internet. *St. Louis Post Dispatch,* p. 3E.

Guilford, D. (1999, August 30). Shell takes banner ads to its critics. *Advertising Age, 70* (36), p. 29.

Herlihy, G. (1999, September 26). Deliver me from spam. *The Atlanta Journal-Constitution,* p. P1.

Hodges, J. (1996, February 26). It's becoming a small World Wide Web after all. *Advertising Age, 67* (6), p. 26.

Hurricanes and football spark otherwise stable month for Web sites. (1999, October 13). *PRNewswire* [Online]. Available: http://biz.yahoo.com/prnews/991013/va_pc_data_1.html (1999, October 13).

Hutheesing, N. (1996, May 20). An online gamble. *Forbes,* p. 288.

Hyland, T. (1998, February 2). Web advertising: A year of growth. *Advertising Age* supplement, *Online Media Strategies for Advertising,* p. A20.

Johnson, B. (1998, October 19). MSN Sidewalk nets $26 million in ad sales. *Advertising Age, 69* (42), p. 70.

Katz, F. (1999, March 7). Portal craze was '98 news; now it's all about content. *The Atlanta Journal-Constitution,* p. H1.

Kelly, K. J. (1996, November 4). Classifieds prove to be a gold mine for online outlets. *Advertising Age,* pp. S23, S27.

The Kelsey Group: Local business market turns to the Web. (1999, June 29). *NUA Surveys, e-mail newsletter* [Online]. Available: http://nua.ie/surveys

Lorge, S. (1999, August). Banner ads vs. e-mail marketing. *Sales and Marketing Management, 151* (15) p. 15.

Maddox, K. (1999, January 4). Warner Bros. Online launches targeted ad package. *Advertising Age, 70* (1), p. 16.

McGinty, R. (1997, March 3). Marketers see Web games as perfect fit for their ads. *Advertising Age, 68* (9), p. 26.

Miller, L. (1999, February 28). Junk e-mailer vows to clean up the Net. *USA Today.com* [Online]. Available: http://www.usatoday.com/life/cyber/tech/cta681.htm (1999, October 15).

Morton, J. (1999, May). A looming threat to newspaper advertising. *American Journalism Review, 21* (4) p. 88.

Napoli, L. (1996). Omnicom boutique investments mark turning point for advertising on the Web. *New York Times on the Web* [Online]. Available: http://search.nytimes.com/Web/docsroot/library/cyber/week/1018omnicom.html

Napoli, L. (1999, January 25). Newspapers acquire online classifieds network. *The New York Times on the Web* [Online]. Available: http://nytimes.com/search (1999, February 19).

Neff, J. (1999, March 15). Internet could see more Web site sponsorships. *Advertising Age, 70* (11), pp. s6, s8.

NetCreations. (1997, Winter). *The Silicon Alley Reporter,* pp. 8, 22.

Outing, S. (1997, June 28). Regional Web ad program. *Editor & Publisher,* p. 42.

Pashupati, K., & Raman, P. (1999). Web banner ads on India's online newspapers: Who's talking, and to whom? *Proceedings of the American Academy of Advertising,* pp. 87–88.

Resnick, R. (1997, February). Marketing riddle. *Internet World,* [Online]. Available: http://pubs.iworld.com

Riedman, P. (1998a, September 7). Expanded games add stickiness to portal sites. *Advertising Age, 69* (36), p. 33.

Riedman, P. (1998b, September 21). Talk City raises $34 mil, signs marketing pacts. *Advertising Age, 69* (38), p. 40.

Shachtman, N. (1998, June 29). Services vie to handle direct e-mail pitches. *Advertising Age, 69* p. 38.

Siegel, A., & Zolli, A. (1999, May 10). Portal envy. *Advertising Age, 70,* pp. 50, 54.

Stone, B. (1998, November 23). An icon from our sponsor. *Newsweek,* p. 71.

Tedeschi, B. (1998a, August 21). A growing ad strategy: "Click to Win!" *The New York Times on the Web* [Online]. Available: http://nytimes.com/search (1999, February 19).

Tedeschi, B. (1998b, December 8). Marketing by e-mail: Sales tool or spam? *The New York Times on the Web* [Online]. Available: http://nytimes.com/search (1999, February 19).

Tedeschi, B. (1998c, September 13). Is coupon clicking the next advertising trend? *The New York Times on the Web* [Online]. Available: http://nytimes.com/search (1999, February 19).

The top twenty-five unsung heroes of the Net. (1997, December 8). *Interactive Week* [Online]. Avaliable: http://www.zdnetnet.com/intweek/ (1998, January 14).

Vadlamudi, P. (1997, October 28). For sale: Classified ads are online moneymaker. *Investor's Daily*, p. A9.

Vonder Haar, S. (1999a, October 11). Classifieds carry e-mail. *Interactive Week, 6* (20), p. 31.

Vonder Haar, S. (1999b, May 31). E-mailing lists: Next big thing. *Interactive Week, 6* (22), p. 25.

Vonder Haar, S. (1999c, July 19). Infomercials coming to e-mail. *Interactive Week, 6* (29), p. 40.

Vonder Haar, S. (1999d, June 14). Repeat Web-business registers. *Interactive Week, 6* (24), p. 46.

Vonder Haar, S. (1999e, June 14). Web promos start from scratch. *Interactive Week, 6* (24), p. 1.

Why Internet advertising. (1997, May 5). *Media-Week, 7* (18), pp. S8–S13.

Williamson, D. A. (1997, June 16). Study shows banners increase brand awareness. *Advertising Age*, p. 42.

Zbar, J. D. (1999, October 25). Marketers buoy brands with e-mail newsletters. *Advertising Age, 70* (42) p. 74.

Chapter 5

Web Ratings
and Measurement

ONLINE AD TRACKING
AUDIENCE DEMOGRAPHIC INFORMATION
RATINGS DATA AND MEASUREMENT
    Counting Ad Exposures
    Web Auditors and Ad Service Companies
MEASUREMENT STANDARDS AND ONLINE ADVERTISING ASSOCIATIONS
ZAPPING CYBERSPACE INVADERS

Advertisers are faced with many new issues as they move their promotions from traditional media to the Internet. Their most pressing concerns are knowing where they should place their ads, which sites draw their target audience, whether their ads appeared on the Web as contracted, and how many people saw their banner.

These concerns are easily addressed when advertising in print or on a broadcast medium. Print media have reliable audience data, ad placement is verified with tearsheets, and estimates of exposure are based on accurate circulation figures. The broadcast media also have reliable demographic data and program ratings, commercial placement is verified by station logs, and exposure is measured based on listener and viewership data.

But on the Internet, these tried and true measures do not exist in a finished form. There are many companies that provide advertisers with campaign management assistance, audience demographic data, Web site ratings, and number of Web site visitors. However, the methods used to obtain the needed information vary from company to company. Lacking industry standardization, each company employs its own unique method of data collection.

This chapter examines online campaign management strategies, audience data collection methods, and Web site ratings analyses. The chapter will discuss each of these advertiser concerns, examine different data collection methods, and take a look at the third-party companies providing the data. These topics are followed by a discussion about efforts to standardize how audience and advertising data are collected and measured. Finally, the avoidance of advertising on the Web by zapping will be considered.

ONLINE AD TRACKING

Managing an online advertising campaign is much more time consuming than buying space and tracking placement in traditional media. Tracking online ad placement can be a nightmare compared to tracking traditionally placed ads. Television and radio stations provide advertisers and agencies with **station logs** verifying that commercials were inserted correctly and aired at the contracted times. Printed newspapers and magazines send copies of ads (**tearsheets**) from the original issues as testimony of ad placement. Rotating banners and a lack of a standard method of verifying online runs makes the tracking process very time intensive and difficult. Unless they watch every Web page on which their ad appears for every minute of the day, advertisers have no way of knowing if their rotating banner really did rotate as specified or if their banner appeared for a specific amount of time somewhere within a large Web site. Advertisers have to rely on the word of the Web site managers as to whether the advertising contract was carried out correctly. Online campaign managers are forced to call or e-mail each Web site operator to verify that banner ads are placed as ordered, to confirm the number of times rotated ads appeared, and to check on other placement concerns. Additionally, unreliable methods of audience measurement and inadequate reach and frequency comparisons to other media and across Web sites make online campaign management an even more cumbersome process. Online campaigns average one employee for every $150,000 in billing, while traditional agencies require one employee for every $1 million billed (Maddox & Bruner, 1998).

Verification of online ad placement and audience reach and standardized tracking systems are way behind those in place for traditional media, leaving Web site operators and advertising buyers to blindly sell and purchase online space. The collective cry for guidance in selling, buying, and tracking cyberads has been answered by new media placement services and Internet advertising networks. Since many of these companies also supply audience demographic and ratings data, they will be introduced later in this chapter.

AUDIENCE DEMOGRAPHIC INFORMATION

For advertisers to know whether they are getting their money's worth of exposures, they need to know about the people who see their ad. Knowing how many people see an ad is just one measure—it alone is not enough to make the best advertising buy. It is crucial that advertisers know who their customers are, what they like, how they spend their leisure time, and other personal characteristics.

Cookies are one of the most commonly used methods of collecting audience data. In addition to using cookies, which many Web users feel violate their privacy, Web sites ask users to voluntarily provide demographic data. Many users readily fill out online forms, especially if it means a discounted price or some other perk as a result of their cooperation.

The Internet offers the promise of very accurate audience data because each person who accesses a page does so through a personal computer or appliance like Web TV that is connected to the Web through an **Internet Service Provider** (**ISP**). All Web surfing activities go through the ISP's server, which can record users' Internet travels. This record can provide data pertaining to which users travel to which sites.

Other targeting strategies include one that is used by *The New York Times.* The paper acquires demographic data entered by the newspaper's online registrants. The paper then charges advertisers a premium for transmitting online ads aimed at a specific audience. The premium fee varies depending on the target group. For example, an advertiser targeting women, regardless of their demographic profiles, would be charged less than an advertiser that is specifically targeting women who have college degrees and are working mothers (Kerwin, 1997).

Box 5.1 ■ HOW USER PROFILING WORKS

Most personal data is collected and analyzed by an ad serving company rather than by the advertiser or the Web site. It is most likely that a Web site's content server is separate from its ad server that actually belongs to a service such as AdForce or DoubleClick. The ad server collects and analyzes personal information and Web site travels to profile customers and a potential audience. The following example from *Red Herring* magazine explains the process of ad serving.

1. Web surfer is on ShoeMart.com looking for 1960s style clogs (ShoeMart.com uses SuperAdService as its ad-serving provider).
2. Both ShoeMart.com and SuperAdService place cookies on the user's PC. ShoeMart.com tells SuperAdService that the user is interested in the 1960s.
3. SuperAdService displays a banner ad on the user's browser for the 1960s bookstore BookMart.com and also updates appropriate notation in its database for the user, BookMart.com, and ShoeMart.com.
4. The next day, the user visits BookMart.com.
5. Before BookMart.com displays its home page, SuperAdService reads the cookie it placed the day before and recalls that the user is into the 1960s scene.
6. SuperAdService tells Bookmart.com about the user's preference. It also updates its own database.
7. While Bookmart.com customizes and then displays its home page to show a book about 1960s shoes, SuperAdService sends the customer a series of banners for ShoeMart.com, as well as for Beatles music at Musicmart.com and BeatMart.com's tours of San Francisco's Haight-Ashbury district. (Zeichick, 2000, p. 216).

Consumer profiling has come under fire from advocacy groups, the Federal Trade Commission (FTC), legislators, and Internet users who are concerned that personal information is being collected without direct consent or knowledge. In late 1999, the FTC and the U.S. Department of Commerce released a plan to notify Web users about what information is being collected and to offer an easy way for consumers to block the collection process. Critics of the plan claim that consumers like profiling because they end up getting ads that are most useful to their needs and tastes and that, if given the chance, it is estimated that only about 4 out of 100 users would actually turn off the profiling function. Consumer advocates, on the other hand, say that consumers would have a fit if they really knew how much data is being collected (Teinowitz, 1999).

RATINGS DATA AND MEASUREMENT

In a medium that is barely half a decade old, the novelty of using it may outshine the need to find out what is really happening with it. Advertisers are jumping on the Internet bandwagon trying to make sure that they do not miss out on a big opportunity. Since demand exists, advertising thrives. Also, the Internet is so different from traditional consumer mass media that measuring the audience may seem like a logistical nightmare.

As recently as 1998, only about 20 percent of the approximately 1,500 advertiser-supported Web sites were audited. Auditing is a function performed by third-party companies that measure audiences and provide in-depth information about various aspects of Web site advertising. Web sites that are audited tend to be the most popular sites. These audited sites receive about 80 percent of Web traffic and thus are able to afford the expense of auditing in order to accurately price their advertising. That situation is changing as more companies get involved in auditing and provide services at many levels and varying costs. These services provide not just ratings, but in-depth information about individual users and traffic patterns that help both large and small sites become more effective and more profitable.

In addition to having information about a Web site content and the types of people who are attracted to particular sites, advertisers need to know how many people travel to a site and thus will be exposed to their banner ad. All other things being equal, an ad placed on a site seen by over 20 million people per month should be more valuable to the advertiser than an ad placed on a site visited by 2 million.

In print media this dimension can be measured by circulation figures that are generated by both the paper or magazine itself (through print runs and copies sold) and by the Audit Bureau of Circulation, a third-party, neutral entity that measures print audience sizes. In television and radio this is equivalent to how many people are tuned to the station or channel at the time the program containing the commercial is shown. In traditional electronic media, this information is provided by a variety of third-party companies, including Nielsen Media Research and Arbitron.

Box 5.2 ■ EDITOR & PUBLISHER SURVEY

Released at the Interactive Newspapers '98 Conference, the Ninth Annual Editor & Publisher Co. survey of over 400 newspaper, magazine, and broadcast news Web sites found that the most critical difference between the top 10 percent revenue-generating newspaper Web sites and everybody else is that the biggest money-makers measure their audience. In addition, it was found that just the presence of audience measurement leads to a 57 percent increase in advertising revenue (Fitzgerald, 1998).

Box 5.3 ■ ONE BILLION HITS

An important milestone was reached during the month of October 1999. An average of one billion Internet hits per day was recorded. The online measuring service Media Metrix Inc., a service that measures Internet usage at home and at work, reported that 32.2 billion page views occurred in the United States. This figure was up over 49 percent from the same month of the previous year (Mack, 1999).

Counting Ad Exposures

Hits   The number of people who access a site or see an ad is commonly referred to as the number of hits. **Hits** are generally defined as the number of times a particular Web page is requested and accessed. But hits are not an accurate measure of the actual number of people that visit a site, because the same person might hit the same page repeatedly in a single visit or on subsequent visits. A small number of visitors may hit a particular page numerous times, giving an inflated perception of the popularity of the site. Another problem is created because ISPs may assign a single IP (Internet Protocol) address to a computer or location, but multiple users may access the Web from that address, such as students using a campus computer lab. Therefore the number of *different* users may be unknown.

Knowing the number of hits a Web site has received is certainly better than knowing nothing or even educated guessing, but in the world of the Web, simply knowing how many pairs of eyes *might* have seen the ad is not that helpful. Because developing an effective Web advertising strategy is a science and art in its infancy, more information is needed to help advertisers find out what works and what they should be paying for the space. For the first few years of the Web's existence, the audience size for a particular Web site was mostly determined by the number of hits the site received in a given time period. Accessing the server log of the site in an offline, cumbersome way often generated the number of hits (Ivins & Reed, 1999).

Caching presents another challenge in determining the number of visitors to a site. The computer often stores a copy of the original page and the browser will retrieve the information from the **cache** (a temporary storage area on the hard drive) rather than the Web site's server. When a Web site visitor returns to a Web page that has been visited during the same Internet session, the server does not record the second hit even though it is a repeat visit or second exposure (Dreze & Zufryden, 1998).

There are types of Web searching software that include automated searchers (**robots, spiders,** and **sniffers**) that travel the Web looking for information. Each time these automated searchers land on a site, they register a hit, although in fact a human pair of eyes never saw the site. Even though automated searchers represent only about 5 percent of the total number of hits, their role still can confuse the overall picture (Edmonston, 1995).

There is often talk of reconciliation of the hit-based ratings generated by ratings companies and server log analysis. Actually, these numbers can be very different because server logs include a Web site's traffic that originates from outside the United States, which may be as much as 40 percent of the site traffic. Audience measurement performed by some companies (e.g., Media Metrix) only monitors U.S.-based usage (Ivins & Reed, 1999).

Click-Throughs   Many people who are involved in advertising on the Web believe that the best measure of advertising response is the click-through rate. The advantage of this measure as compared to measuring hits or unique visitors is that it shows when a visitor has expressed interest in the advertising by taking an action.

Using the click-through as a measure of effectiveness has sparked the debate of how effectiveness in Web advertising should be measured. Some believe that a click-through is not an accurate predictor of conversion (leading to a sale). This notion has led to products that can track user behavior beyond the click.

Not surprisingly, a survey conducted by the Association of National Advertisers in 1998 concluded that lack of accurate measurement and difficulty tracking return on investment are cited as the biggest barriers to buying online media (Cleland, 1998).

Web Auditors and Ad Service Companies

In an effort to simplify matters, many research companies have begun measuring online audiences and providing assistance to online advertisers and marketers, and new research and online ad servicing companies have been created for similar purposes. However, different means of data collection and audience measurement often create more problems and dilemmas than are being solved.

A number of companies have received attention for their efforts in Web advertising. Some of these companies perform a variety of services that range from connecting advertisers with Web sites, buying banner spots, tracking ad performance, collecting audience data, and providing Web site ratings and number of site visitors. What becomes problematic, however, is that many of these companies use varying techniques to arrive at their figures. Lack of standardized data collection methods lead to contradictory reports that can often confuse advertisers and Web site providers.

For example, Media Metrix and Nielsen/NetRatings are perhaps the best known and widely used companies for reporting Web site visitation. Media Metrix uses patented metering methodology to measure actual Internet audience usage behavior. The data are collected in real time and the information is analyzed click by click, page by page, and minute by minute.

Nielsen/NetRatings service also provides a number of data reports that give information about Web usage and e-commerce. Nielsen also gives a report of the top Web properties on the Internet. However, Nielsen's data collection methods differ from those used by Media Metrix. Nielsen generates their report based on usage by its sample of households that have Internet access and use the operating systems Windows 95/98/NT or MacOS 8 or higher. The sample is comprised of fourteen thousand users and the data is compiled in real time. The service provides an in-depth look at online campaigns, tracks usage data on banners and other advertising, and provides demographics and other audience data (Maddox, 1999a).

Table 5.1 and Table 5.2 both report the top 10 Web sites in October 1999 in terms of the number of visitors. The figures in Table 5.1 were provided by Media Metrix and the numbers in Table 5.2 by Nielsen. The differences between the tables illustrate what can come about when different audience measuring techniques are used.

The Media Metrix ranking in Table 5.1 is based upon the **unduplicated audience** that reaches a site. In other words, these data show the number of different visitors (or unique visitors) that land on a Web site. This type of measure is similar to **cumulative audience** in broadcasting. Media Metrix uses a sample of fifty thousand people and measures Internet use behavior both at work and at home. The company evaluates **Web properties,** which are either single sites or a consolidation of sites that fall under one brand or common ownership.

When the rankings between the two tables are compared, some discrepancies are evident. First, Media Metrix combines the MSN (Microsoft Network) site with the other Microsoft sites to yield a property that ranks third. Nielsen/NetRatings

**TABLE 5.1   Media Metrix Ranking of Top
10 Web Sites, October 1999**

Rank	Web Properties	Unique Visitors (000)
1	AOL sites	53,373
2	Yahoo! sites	40,134
3	Microsoft sites	37,737
4	Lycos	29,227
5	Go Network	21,729
6	Excite@Home	15,021
7	Amazon	12,902
8	Time Warner Online	12,475
9	Go2Net Network	11,326
10	Bluemountainarts.com	10,961

**TABLE 5.2   Nielsen Ranking of Top 10
Web Sites, October 1999**

Rank	Web Properties	Unique Visitors (000)
1	AOL sites	40,391
2	Yahoo!	36,808
3	MSN	24,775
4	Lycos Network	23,754
5	Go Network	16,970
6	Microsoft	12,106
7	Excite@Home	11,972
8	Time Warner	11,330
9	Amazon	10,049
10	Blue Mt. Arts	9,331

separates MSN from the other Microsoft sites, yielding a third rank for MSN and a sixth rank for other Microsoft sites. Second, the number of unique visitors does not match. Although both companies rank AOL first, Media Metrix reports 53 million unique visitors whereas Nielsen/NetRatings claim AOL only received slightly over 40 million unique visitors. The same type of discrepancy appears with the Time Warner properties (over 12.4 million according to Media Metrix versus 11.3 million according to Nielsen/NetRatings) and with several others.

The different figures between Media Metrix and Nielsen arise from different definitions of *audience* and different data collection methods. The way each company extrapolates total audience figures from sample data varies enough to yield very different audience ratings and rankings. Media Metrix measures Internet usage when users are at home *or* at work. Nielsen/NetRatings collects Internet activity that occurs in the home because they believe that there is no way to access an appropriate workplace sample. Workplace Internet surfing may be very different from home use; therefore there is much debate over whether it is best to collect Internet activity from the home, from work, or from both places. Obviously, the science of measuring Internet audiences presents many questions that must be resolved (Tedesco, 1999; Vonder Haar, 1999b; Vogelstein, 1999).

Whereas Media Metrix and Nielsen are giants in the field of Internet measurement, WebSideStory is a small auditing company that offers real-time information and reports. The company provides such data as a user's browser type and version, the search engine that referred the user to the monitored site, the user's computer's operating system, and such details as the screen resolution, colors, and size. This type of tracking occurs via a proprietary *super cookie* that is embedded in the user's browser after the user visits a site that has this cookie embedding software installed. Interestingly, WebSideStory does not charge for this auditing service, but generates revenue instead from advertising on Hitbox.com (http://www.hitbox.com), a community site for Webmasters (Roberts-Witt, 1999).

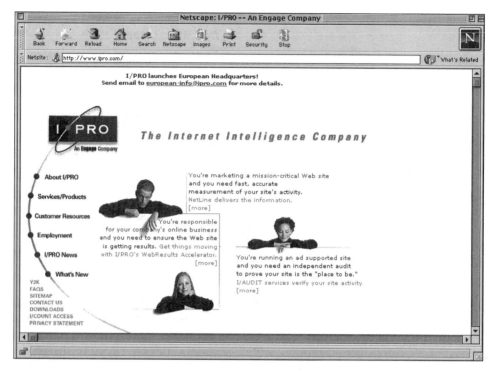

FIGURE 5.1 I/PRO at **http://www.ipro.com/**

Other types of online services provide Web site operators with traffic reports and other information about their sites rather than about their advertising placed on other sites. I/Pro's NetLine (http://www.ipro.com) is a tool that translates data from a Web server into a comprehensive report that site managers can use to optimize site design, improve content, and price banner ads (Figure 5.1). Netline provides the ratings and circulation figures that are needed to calculate the cost of online ads.

Media Metrix, Nielsen/Net Ratings, WebSideStory, and I/Pro specialize in measuring Web site traffic and in providing audience demographic data. These companies directly serve Web site marketers rather than online advertisers. However, they indirectly affect advertisers as their results are used to help marketers sell ad space. Other new online ad servicing companies provide various types of assistance to the online ad industry, especially online advertisers and their agencies.

DoubleClick (http://www.doubleclick.com), is one of the largest advertising brokerage and management services companies and includes auditing services as part of the management package it provides to its customers. Late in 1999 DoubleClick merged with NetGravity (an ad-serving company) and then Abacus Direct (a provider of information products and marketing research services). DoubleClick has emerged as one of the largest Internet advertising networks currently in existence.

On its online "company info" page it claims that "DoubleClick allows advertisers to cut through the clutter generated by the hundreds of thousands of sites on the

Web and deliver their advertising message to their most valuable prospects." The company sells ad space on over 1,500 sites worldwide and provides centralized tracking and campaign management services for its advertisers. DoubleClick's newest addition, DoubleClick Local, targets Web users by their geographic location—either city, state, or region. With the local angle, advertisers can transmit location-specific banners to target shoppers who live in the areas where they have traditional stores. For example, a national chain such as WalMart could advertise local store promotions and addresses to users who live close to one of their stores, but users who do not live within driving distance of WalMart would see a more general banner.

As a result of its merger with NetGravity, one of the leading developers of software used by publishers and advertisers for in-house monitoring of ads and campaigns, DoubleClick can now offer full-service ad management or sell its stand-alone software for self-management. DoubleClick is quite a formidable competitor to others with fewer options (Blankenhorn, 1999; Gilbert, 1999d; Vonder Haar & Guglielmo, 1999).

DoubleClick's merger with Abacus Direct Corporation, seller of consumer catalog purchase information, will put DoubleClick in the forefront of targeting banner ads to users based on their past offline purchases (Tedeschi, 1999).

Engage Media (http://www.engage.com/engagemedia), formerly Flycast Communications, is a San Francisco–based company that specializes in Internet direct response advertising solutions. As opposed to brand advertising that

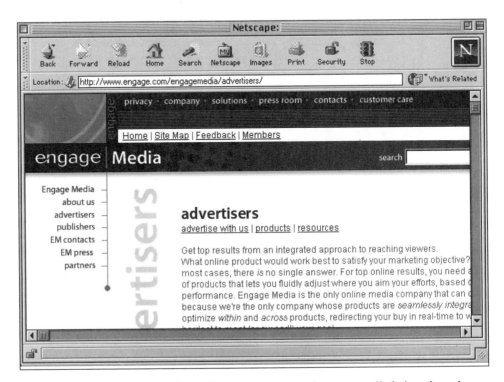

FIGURE 5.2 Engage Media, **http://www.engage.com/engagemedia/advertisers/**

attempts to increase awareness or improves attitudes toward a product, the goal of direct response advertising is behavioral response by the audience. Engage Media believes that the Internet is especially suited for direct response advertising because the results are directly measurable. In other words, when sales are generated from a Web site, Engage measures this through auditing and can report it to the advertiser. Engage also acquires unsold space on a large variety of Web sites and places advertising on them for Engage customers.

The parent company of Engage Media, CMGI, has a new audience targeting service, known as AudienceNet. Using audience data collected by Engage, AudienceNet promises to deliver specific targeted demographic groups to marketers and may become one of DoubleClick's formidable competitors (Vonder Haar, 1999a).

FocaLink Communication's AdKnowledge (http://www.focalink.com/aksystem/index.html) is another Web auditor and Web advertiser consultant. AdKnowledge (Figure 5.3) provides a system that puts its clients in control of their online media dollars. The company works with advertisers interested in both brand awareness and direct response. The AdKnowledge system assists and guides over 200 advertisers in planning, buying, tracking, targeting, reporting, and analyzing their online advertising. AdKnowledge consists of four compo-

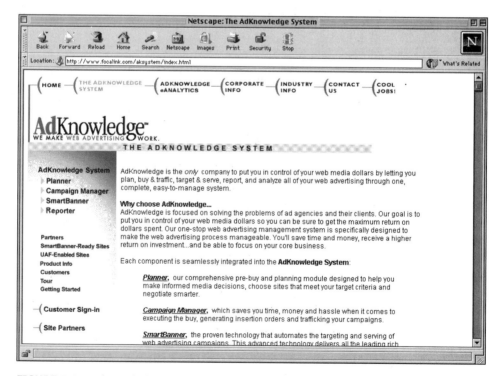

FIGURE 5.3   AdKnowledge, **http://www.adknowledge.com**

nents (MarketMatch Planner, Campaign Manager, Smart Banner, and Reporter) each with its own function.

MarketMatch Planner is an online management tool for planning and evaluating campaigns and guiding advertisers to smart buys. Campaign Manager generates insertion orders and monitors ad placement. SmartBanner automates the targeting process and delivers rich-media formats, and Reporter customizes pre- and postcampaign reports. AdKnowledge's newest component, Administrator, will integrate online advertising purchasing and performance data with clients' existing accounting systems (Bayne, 1998).

MatchLogic (http://www.matchlogic.com) is a firm that provides outsourced ad tracking and targeting services. On its Web site, MatchLogic promotes itself to advertisers, direct marketers, and digital merchants. The company provides "a turn-key solution for creating and managing one-to-one customer relationships in the digital channel." The company focuses on targeting, online measurement, and data asset management to develop custom campaigns based on its clients' needs and objectives. The company also provides clients with ROI (return on investment) information that is expressed in brand awareness, leads, sales, and customer lifetime value.

Whether online ad campaign information is outsourced or tabulated in-house, this information is crucial to advertisers and marketers who need to know if their online efforts are paying off. Advertisers and their agencies are interested in accumulating as much campaign data as possible to measure their return on investment. The number of agencies and advertisers using ad-serving technology is rapidly growing along with the dependence on performance and customer data (Gilbert, 1999b). However, the discrepancies between the results produced by ratings services and other ad service firms create a dilemma for advertisers. Advertisers and Web site operators have no way of knowing which service provides the most accurate data and therefore they do not have reliable information on which to base advertising buys and sales (Roberts-Witt, 1999).

MEASUREMENT STANDARDS AND ONLINE ADVERTISING ASSOCIATIONS

Measurement standards are necessary to allow comparisons among sites. Since companies involved in Web ratings employ different measurement procedures, it is often very difficult to compare cost effectiveness. In addition, Web audience ratings are often based on absolute numbers rather than estimates that are based on samples that may be using an imperfect system of generating the numbers. One Internet expert summed up the state of Web measurement by asserting that ratings numbers "represent a measurement process that is in evolution, but for now has serious shortcomings" (Shaw, 1998, p. 17).

Additionally, burgeoning Web commerce brings the need to support and promote online advertising and to establish ethical standards. The online marketplace attracts diverse companies and a global audience that necessitate a forum for discussion and decision making regarding marketing and advertising on the Web. Several associations specifically tackle the multitude of issues surrounding online advertising.

Coalition for Advertising Supported Information and Entertainment (CASIE) (http://www.casie.com) was founded in May 1994 by the Association of National Advertisers, Inc. (ANA), and the American Association of Advertising Agencies (AAAA). The coalition was organized before the advent of the Web and was initially concerned with interactive television and CD-ROMs but has since switched its focus to the Internet. CASIE's primary functions are to establish media measurement guidelines, judge and present the CASIE awards for best online ads, examine Internet advertising effectiveness, develop industry self-regulation guidelines, monitor federal and state legislation pertaining to the Internet, and standardize banner ad sizes.

Among its interests in online advertising, CASIE is working on ways to standardize Web auditing and measurement. The group is pioneering new and effective means of gathering audience data and attempting to standardize definitions of terms. Advertisers need to know who is being measured (i.e., at-home or at-work audiences), how they are being measured (i.e., by hits or exposures), and exactly what the terms mean (is a robot search a hit or is a hit just a human exposure, what about cached visits, etc.) ("ARF Guides Methods in Measuring Cyberspace," 1996).

A high-profile effort by Future of Advertising Stakeholders (FAST) was begun in late 1998 to accelerate the development of advertising standards on the Web. This group, a mixture of major advertisers, online publishers, interactive advertising agencies, and leading technological companies, has come together in an effort to accelerate standardization of advertising online. The organization is considering three existing forms of audience measurement: ratings services, server logs of site traffic, and third-party ad server reports. The group acknowledges that the process of standardization will take years to resolve ("Web Ad Standards May Not Be FAST in Coming," 1998; Maddox, 1999b; Mand, 1999).

The Internet Advertising Bureau (IAB) (http://www.iab.net) was formed in part because of the intense need to develop a unified code of online advertising. The IAB (Figure 5.4) was organized in 1996 by some of the Web's most influential players, such as Microsoft, Juno Online (http://www.juno.com), and Infoseek (http://www.infoseek.com), which put aside their rivalries for the sake of establishing advertising standards and examining ways to maximize the effectiveness of Internet advertising.

The IAB promotes itself as "the first global not for profit association devoted exclusively to maximizing the use and effectiveness of advertising on the Internet." The association is committed to setting ethical standards for online advertising, developing guidelines for self-regulation, professional development, shaping the direction of the industry, and promoting the Internet as an advertising vehicle.

In 1998 the IAB merged with The Internet Local Advertising and Commerce Association (ILAC), a nonprofit organization primarily devoted to local Internet market issues. ILAC's goals include establishing standard directory search cate-

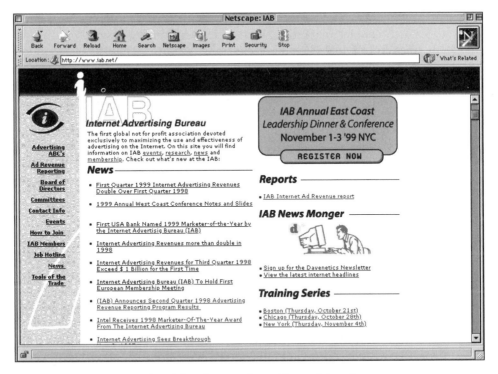

FIGURE 5.4   Internet Advertising Bureau, **http://www.iab.net**

gories and developing standards and strategies to ease advertising buys across multiple, local Internet products ("Internet Ad Associations to Combine," 1998; "New Internet Association," 1997).

The Internet Direct Marketing Bureau (IDMB) (http://www.idmb.org/mission.asp) is a trade group formed in Fall 1998 to cover issues not dealt with by either the IAB or the Direct Marketing Association (DMA). Where IAB is primarily concerned with advertising and DMA with online commerce, the IDMB will focus on "the things that happen between the time an impression is served and the time a customer makes a purchase in the relationship cycle" (Maddox, 1998). According to IDMB's Web site, the organization's primary purposes are as follows:

1. to serve as an information resource and a collective voice for vendors and customers of Internet marketing products and services,
2. to define the products, services and companies which comprise the Internet marketing space,
3. to establish best practices, guidelines and standards for effective and ethical use of direct marketing products and services on the Internet,
4. to educate the Internet marketing trade and traditional marketers who will use our services about the services we offer and how they are priced and measured.

The Advertising Research Foundation (ARF) promotes high-quality business and consumer marketing, advertising, and media research by providing guidelines and standards, and objective and impartial technical advice and expertise to its members. Because of its size, it is able to undertake research projects that individual advertisers or agencies could not afford.

The Advertising Standards Alliance was formed in 1999 for the purpose of proposing solutions to a number of online advertising-related concerns, including audience measurement and online privacy. The alliance is made up of 11 companies including 24/7 Media, DoubleClick, Engage Technologies, and Real Media. Their primary goal is to provide a forum for technology-related companies to create online advertising standards and a uniform approach to audience measurement (Vonder Haar, 1999a).

ZAPPING CYBERSPACE INVADERS

All the effort going into online ad targeting, customer profiling, and standardizing ratings measurement could be for naught if people zap out or block online ads. Avoiding commercials and ads appearing on traditional media is not a new concept, but avoiding them on the Internet is a unique phenomenon.

People have been trying to block out advertising on television for many years. Often people will say that they prefer to record their favorite shows on videotape. Taping a show allows them to time shift (that is, watch the show at their convenience), but it also allows them the ability to zip or fast forward quickly through the commercials. A one-hour show can usually be viewed in about 45 minutes when the commercials are zipped. Some videocassette recorders have been designed with special controls that allow the user to pause recording for 30 seconds at a time to skip individual commercials when recording a program from a commercial network or station. These special-model VCRs have met with very little success. Other devices have been tried, but none have really caught on. Despite the available hardware to avoid recording commercials and the ability to zip through commercials once they are taped, only a small percentage of the population actually bothers to avoid commercials regularly. At least in commercial television, advertising seems to be about as easy to avoid as paying taxes.

Billions of dollars have been spent for advertising on the Web. Rarely does a popular site exist that does not have some form of advertising on it. Web industry officials have been known to draw comparisons between the Web and commercial television. They contend that if users want the free content that the Web has to offer, users must tolerate the advertising that pays for it (Flynn, 1999).

While ads on television can be irritating, ads on the Web can be infuriating. Web users with slower modems or connections might have to wait 10 seconds or more while a page with a bandwidth hogging animated banner loads slowly. This delay encourages impatient visitors to abort a page before the banner has even loaded (Gilbert, 1999b). Many Web pages are designed so that the content of the page does not show until sometime after the banner is fully loaded and showing on the screen. This reality led to the creation of a number of programs designed to prevent ads from even appearing on users' screens. In addition, some of these programs can even prevent advertisers from collecting information from users by interfering with cookies ("Mad about Online Ads," 1999).

Programs that block ads and are available to Internet users include At Guard, Internet Junkbuster Proxy, Intermute, and Web Washer. In addition to blocking ads on Web sites, these programs offer a side benefit. When ads are blocked, sites load faster—generally because files with ads that have sophisticated graphics such as animation or other type of bandwidth-grabbing rich media will load more slowly than files that just have text.

A controversial filtering software program entitled Cybersitter marketed by Solid Oak Software has two filtering functions. The program was designed to block indecent Web sites from being accessed by children. Recently a file was added to the program that will block advertising banners at any Web site. The program can discriminate between ads and content-related graphics on a Web page.

This program and others like it are drawing criticism from some Web activist groups. The issue is that filtering programs of any kind may (at least according to the user groups such as PeaceFire) encroach on the Web site author's free speech (McWilliams, 1998). Web site operators are also annoyed by ad blocking. When an ad is blocked, it is not downloaded from the advertiser's server. When the ad is not downloaded from the server, the Web site operator may not get paid for delivering or serving the ad to the site visitor.

Some Web site publishers have expressed strong sentiment against ad blockers. A vice president of Channelseek (which offers an online guide to live Web events) has stated that ad blocking is like "a shoplifter coming and taking your money away." The company has created a software code that will prevent anyone who uses an ad-blocking program from even logging onto the Channelseek site. Some analysts, however, feel that the most effective ad blocker that Web site visitors can use is the one "between their ears" ("The Hand That Feeds the Internet," 1999). Obviously, the issue of ad blocking will continue to create heated debate as more and more advertisers seek to use the Internet to reach audiences.

The ad blocking programs and products like them are enjoying brisk sales. The Web Washer program sold about one million copies in 1998. But the number of programs sold to block ads is small compared to the total number of Web users in this country, which has been estimated at 80 to 100 million. Therefore, the percentage of the total audience that can block ads is probably about one percent.

SUMMARY

The World Wide Web is a new medium that offers fresh opportunities and challenges to advertisers. One of the major challenges is accurate measurement of the audience. Although the ability exists to count every visitor to every site with an advertisement on it, there are differing opinions about how to measure exposure to the advertising. Advertising professionals disagree about what is most important as a measure of advertising effectiveness: hits, click-throughs, or actual sales.

There are several companies that regularly measure traffic at popular Web sites. These companies generate lists of the top properties on the Web, but they do show discrepancies regarding how the audience is measured. Many companies are getting involved in auditing Web site advertising. This process gives specific information such as traffic patterns of site visitors and demographic information to advertisers that need to know more about how their advertising is performing on the Web.

A major problem with Web advertising is a lack of measurement standards. This prevents advertisers from comparing cost effectiveness across the Web. Several professional groups are involved in efforts to provide standard definitions for Web advertising terms and guidelines for measuring effectiveness.

Media placement services and Internet advertising networks provide clients with campaign management tools. They match advertisers with appropriate online venues, they guide clients to effective online buys and placement, and they monitor costs, number of impressions and click-throughs, and banner effectiveness among other campaign management services.

Internet advertising associations are offering guidelines and setting standards for new advertising outlets. These associations are tackling such issues as proper measurement techniques, standardized banner sizes, privacy, and regulation.

As the proliferation of Web advertising continues, companies are designing software programs that will filter out advertising. The motivation behind these programs is not only to block the advertising message, but to allow users to speed up their Web surfing while eliminating slow-loading ads from the Web pages they request.

Discussion Questions

1. How does the Internet offer the promise of accurate ratings measurement?
2. Why do you think that various measurement companies follow different procedures and data collection methods?
3. What are the shortcomings of current Web measurement practices?
4. Should people be allowed to block out Web advertisements? Why or why not?
5. Why do certain groups express strong sentiment against ad blockers?
6. Why aren't simple hits an effective measurement of the number of visitors to a site?
7. Discuss ways to make it easier to track online placement.
8. In what ways are services such as DoubleClick important to their clients?
9. What are the main roles of the Internet associations? In what ways do IAB, IDMB, and CASIE differ and in what ways are they similar? Why are these associations important to the Internet world?

Chapter Activities

1. Research several companies that conduct Web measurement and compare the services they offer. Examine the different Internet measurement techniques employed by each.
2. Surf through the Web and select banners that you would like to block and those you would like to see. Determine whether you feel it would be better to block out all ads or to see all of the ads. What ads would you miss? What ads could you live without? How would you develop a system for selecting which ads to see and which to block?

References

ARF guides methods in measuring cyberspace, (1996, February 19). *Advertising Age,* p. c11.

Banner ads increase audience reach. (1999, October 8). *New York Times.* As cited by *NUA Internet Surveys* [Online]. Available: http://www.nua.ie/surveys/index

Bayne, K. M. (1998, June 8). AdKnowledge rolls out Web ad evaluation tool. *Advertising Age* [Online]. Available: http://adage.com/interactive/articles/19980608/article3.html

Blankenhorn, D. (1999, March 1). AdKnowledge goes beyond clicks to measurable results. *Advertising Age,* p. 4.

Cleland, K. (1998, August 3). Marketers want solid data on value of Internet ad buys. *Advertising Age,* p. 18.

Dreze, X., and Zufryden, F. (1998). Is Internet advertising ready for prime time? *Journal of Advertising Research, 38* (3), pp. 7–18.

Edmonston, J. (1995, August). When is a Web ad simply too costly? *Business Marketing,* p. 18.

Fitzgerald, M. (1998, Febuary 14). Measuring Web site traffic. *Editor & Publisher.* p. 51.

Flynn, L. (1999, June 7). Software ad blockers challenge web industry. *The New York Times on the Web* [Online]. Available: http://search.nytimes.com/search/daily

Gilbert, J. (1999a, July 19). DoubleClick clicks with NetGravity. *Advertising Age, 70* (30), p. 38.

Gilbert, J. (1999b, June 28). Industry eyes counting banners a different way. *Advertising Age,* p. 42.

Hoffman, K. (1998, May 4). Ratings partnership merges data from sites and users. *Inter-*

net World [Online]. Available: http://www.internetworld.com/

Internet ad associations to combine. (1998, June 17). *Internet Advertising Bureau* [Online]. Available: http://www.iab.net/news/merge_source.html (1999, September 20).

Ivins, B., & Reed, T. (1999, January 18). Comparing audience to server logs. *Advertising Age,* p. 35.

Kerwin, A. M. (1997, July 14). "NY Times" Web site lets advertisers get personal. *Advertising Age,* p. 35.

Mack, J. (1999, November 22). A Net record: 1 billion page views per day. *ZDNet News* [Online]. Available: http://news.excite.com/news/zd/991122/16/

Mad about online ads. (1999, July 5). *Newsweek,* p. 66.

Maddox, K. (1998, August 10). Online direct marketers will form new trade group. *Advertising Age, 69* (32), pp. 18, 20.

Maddox, K. (1999a, March 22). Nielsen, NetRatings roll out new service. *Advertising Age,* p. 40.

Maddox, K. (1999b, March 8). FAST panel proposes measurement guidelines. *Advertising Age,* p. 42.

Maddox, K., & Bruner, R. E. (1998, January 26). New services automate online media planning. *Advertising Age,* p. 38.

Mand, A. (1999, May 3). The FAST track. *Brandweek, 40* (18), pp. IQ22–OQ28.

McWilliams, B. (1998, February 12). Internet filtering software now blocks ad banners. *PC World News Radio.*

New Internet association to serve local advertising and commerce marketplace is holding organizational meeting. (1997, February 20). *Business Wire* [Online]. Available: http://www.businesswire.com/

Roberts-Witt, S. (1999, May 3). Reinventing the hit counter. *Internet World* [Online]. Available: http://www.internetworld.com/

Shaw, R. (1998, March 2). At least there are no Web sweeps (yet). *Electronic Media*, p. 17.

Tedesco, R. (1999, March 29). Net ratings war explodes. *Broadcasting and Cable Magazine*, p. 58.

Teinowitz, I. (1999, November 15). Consumers to be notified about profiling. *Advertising Age, 70* (47), p. 52.

The hand that feeds the Internet. (1999, June 22). *The New York Times on the Web* [Online]. Available: http://search.nytimes.com/search/daily/

Vogelstein, F. (1999, April 5). Rating Web sites. *U.S. News and World Report*, p. 50.

Vonder Haar, S. (1999a, November 22). New group aims to tackle ad standards. *Interactive Week, 6* (29), p. 22.

Vonder Haar, S. (1999b, March 22). Web ratings rivalry re-ignites. *Interactive Week*, p. 11.

Vonder Haar, S., & Guglielmo C. (1999, July 19). Let's make a deal. *Interactive Week, 6* (29), p. 22.

Web ad standards may not be FAST in coming. (1998, November 2). *Interactive Week online* [Online]. Available: http://www.zdnet.com/intweek/stories/

Zeichick, A. (2000, January). Ad serving explained. *Red Herring, 74*, p. 216.

Chapter 6

Agency Presence Online

AGENCIES AND CYBERSPACE

Advertising agencies are adapting to an online environment. They recognize that **interactivity** is here to stay and they have placed themselves in the forefront of Web development, advertising sales, pricing, and audience measurement. Additionally, traditional campaign strategies and management are challenged in the move to cyberspace. Online technology allows advertising agencies to sell themselves to potential clients and it gives their clients a new means of selling their goods and services to a global marketplace.

This chapter discusses how advertising agencies and other institutions connected to advertising have adapted to the cyberenvironment by restructuring their day-to-day operations, hiring Web designers and technical specialists, purchasing independent interactive firms, and incorporating other strategies that build online readiness. Next, online campaign management is discussed followed by the rise of Internet advertising associations and their role in the online world.

Advertising System

Advertisers are a part of a larger interacting system that includes the government, competition, advertising agencies, media, and research suppliers.

Box 6.1 ■ ADVERTISING SYSTEM

In their text *Advertising Management*, Aaker, Batra, and Myers (1992, p. 2) offer the following illustration as an example of the advertising system:

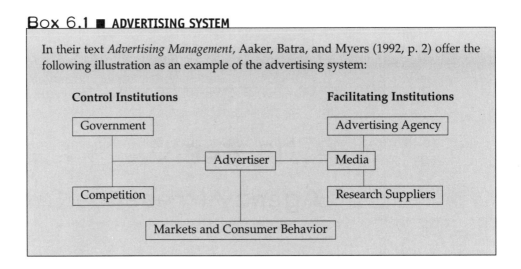

Typically, in an non-online world the advertiser deals with all of the institutions involved in the advertising system. Advertisers are assisted by ad agencies, media, and research suppliers. Agencies and research companies help advertisers identify opportunities, provide marketing and advertising data, test advertising ideas, create campaigns, and buy media time. The media are central to the process, as they offer airtime and print space for message distribution (Aaker et al., 1992).

Advertisers are externally controlled by the government and competition. The government sets forth regulations concerning the advertiser's products, services, and advertising. Competitors' reactions and market moves also affect advertising decisions.

The target market or consumers facilitate and control an advertiser. Without an existing or potential market, there would be no need for advertising; thus the market acts as a facilitator. Yet at the same time consumers' behavior and reactions to products and services dictate advertising strategy.

In the online world of advertising, the relationships and interactions between these institutions are changing. Government regulation and intervention is practically nonexistent on the Internet and thus the government does not have the same control over Internet advertising as it does over non-online advertising.

Competition is fierce as many new companies offer e-commerce and there are often very few distinguishing characteristics between competing **dot.coms.** Advertiser's relationships with facilitating institutions are also in flux. Advertising agencies have taken on new functions to accommodate online needs, and new interactive shops compete for the advertiser's business.

The Internet is more than just a new place to advertise. Its very existence is changing the interactions and relationships among the institutions that facilitate and control advertising. As Internet advertising matures, a new system unique to the online realm will no doubt develop (Aaker et al., 1992).

Advertising Agencies in an Online World

Thousands of advertising agencies of all sizes and from all geographic locations have developed Web sites of their own. DDB Needham Worldwide (http://www. ddbn.com), Mad Dogs & Englishmen (http://www.maddogadv.com), Starcom (http://www.starcommedia.com), TBWA/Chiat Day (http://www.tbwachiat.com), and Grey Advertising (http://www.grey.com/index3.htm) are just a few of many agencies with a dynamic Web presence. Many agencies have a Web site for their global parent company with additional sites for specific geographic locations and/or divisions. For example, Young & Rubicam's San Francisco office (http:// www.yrsf.com/home.html) has a Web site that is separate from Young & Rubicam Inc. (http://www.yr.com).

Agencies have many types of Web sites. Some are serious minded whereas others are fun and lighthearted. Visitors to highly diverse agency sites may find client lists, agency background, staff photos and biographies, and interactive games and quizzes. On the Ogilvy & Mather Web site (http://www.ogilvy.com), visitors can click on the Our Work link for clips of television commercials and displays of banner ads created by the agency. Leo Burnett's Ideas also displays an Our Works section that presents its advertisements that appear in print, television, and other media (http://www.leoburnett.com).

While thousands of advertising agencies of all different sizes have posted Web sites of their own, by 1998 only half of the top 10 revenue-grossing agencies had done so (Carmichael, 1998). A TBWA Chiat/Day/Venice spokesperson claims that before an agency attempts to meet its clients' online advertising needs, it should first develop an effective Web presence of its own. "We have to experiment on ourselves before we can ask our clients to get involved" (Riedman, 1996, p. 25).

Interactive Departments   The desire to jump on the Internet bandwagon has prompted many agencies to update their corporate structure by creating **interactive departments.** Ogilvy & Mather was years ahead of the times when it established an interactive department in the early 1980s. The agency is still recognized as one of the top interactive, new media firms. Other large agencies such as McCann-Erickson Worldwide (http://www.mccann.com) and BBDO (http://www. bbdo.com) were also early to open separate operating units for interactive media. Although Ogilvy & Mather was a pioneer in interactivity and many large agencies have followed in its footsteps, it is generally recognized that the medium- and small-sized agencies have led the way to online advertising. Small agencies are generally less rigidly structured and more flexible in terms of organizational functioning and thus can quickly add interactive components. New staff experienced in interactive technology can be quickly hired and are more easily integrated into a small agency's corporate structure than in a large agency (Gleason & Williamson, 1996; Williamson, 1995).

Grey Advertising's independent media service company, MediaCom, opened a new division for the purpose of integrating traditional and interactive media campaigns. MediaCom specializes in cross-media campaigns, which can include any combination of print, television, radio, Internet, and broadband digital media. MediaCom's clients are those who want to expand their media mix. "Many clients will have started operating in the traditional world—TV, print—and know they should be doing something online," commented a MediaCom senior vice president (Gilbert, 1999c, p. 68).

Box 6.2 ■ INTERACTIVE AGENCY SUCCESS STORY

Way back in 1995, a guy and a married couple with a vision of helping companies come alive online set up shop with their Mac computer. They called their new interactive enterprise Agency.com (http://www.agency.com). British Airways, one of their first clients, asked the start-up to redesign the airline's site. Rather than just giving the site a facelift, Agency.com suggested the company rethink its online business model. As a result British Airways ended up with an online ticketing system and a site that focused on "new ways to use interactive technology to expand market share, reduce costs, improve efficiency, and deliver great customer satisfaction."

Agency.com's success with British Airways led to new online projects with companies such as Compaq, Nike, Sprint, and Texaco. Agency.com quickly became known for its outstanding work. *Adweek* named it one of the top 10 interactive agencies for 1996.

Agency.com caught the attention of OmnicomGroup (http://www.omnicomgroup.com), a marketing communication company. OmnicomGroup acquired a 40 percent share in Agency.com, so the interactive start-up now had the money it needed to expand its enterprise—and expand it did.

Over the next 3 years, Agency.com acquired or purchased stakes in 12 interactive agencies around the world. Currently, Agency.com employs over 1,000 people internationally. As the agency has grown and changed, so has its mission. The company has changed from "helping businesses bring their business online to empowering people and organizations to gain competitive advantage through interactive relationships," which it does through a discipline it calls Interactive Relationship Management.

Pretty good work for a guy, a couple, and their Mac computer ("History," 1999).

Interactive Shops   While many agencies are investing in new equipment and personnel and are establishing interactive departments, as of 1996 only about 4 out of 10 agencies had their own teams of **Web designers** and **technical programmers.** Many agencies prefer to **outsource** their online work to stand-alone interactive/Web firms rather than hire their own personnel. Advertisers also contract directly with Web specialists rather than with traditional agencies (Forrester Research, Inc., 1996).

Many in the advertising business are discovering that neither the traditional agencies nor the new interactive firms can totally meet their needs. Many new media/interactive companies are launched by entrepreneurs with expertise in Web design and technology but not necessarily in advertising and marketing. Conversely, many advertising experts lack Web experience. In today's world where companies are involved in both the online and offline commerce, marketing and advertising needs go beyond the capabilities of traditional agencies. As a Forrester Research analyst points out, "Marketers are really looking for Internet business strategy. That's the first thing they've got to figure out. That's a whole different thing than advertising/marcom strategy" (Williamson, 1999, p. s26). As a result, online ventures are turning to Web developers and e-commerce strategists before they call an advertising agency. Similar sentiments were reported by Forrester Research, which found clients are only "marginally satisfied with their agencies' online efforts" (Riedman, 1999).

Spurred by the need for personnel with expertise in advertising and online media, many larger agencies have purchased smaller **interactive agencies** and incorporated them into their larger operations. For example, OmnicomGroup spent over $10 million to purchase seven small Web design companies. These acquisitions merged the best of the advertising and Web worlds and helped legitimize the Internet as an advertising medium.

There is some debate among industry experts as to whether interactive shops should be linked to traditional agencies and, if so, whether they should keep the agency's name. Many interactive shops see their projects as farther reaching than just advertising. Interactive agencies may be involved with media buying, banner development, and other online ad functions, and many may also develop Web sites and be involved in other technologically sophisticated endeavors such as e-commerce. Interactive experts are concerned that traditional agencies have not been able to move forward from their traditional ways of conducting business. Further concerns regard clients' perceptions of traditional agencies as outlets for traditional advertising but not for online efforts. Thus, stand-alone interactive shops may have a competitive advantage over those associated with traditional agencies. Yet, others claim that interactive shops do not have the capabilities to offer clients a full range of services and thus need to be tied to a traditional agency.

Young & Rubicam recognized that putting interactive divisions of larger agencies up against independent interactive specialists is not always the best strategy. Y & R sold off its interactive division, Brand Dialogue, which only brought in $7.2 million in revenue in 1998, to start-up boutique Clarant Worldwide Corporation (now Luminant Worldwide Corporation, http://www.luminant.com). Y & R retained the rights to the Brand Dialogue name and will end up owning 13 percent of Luminant.

Y & R is not alone in its approach to interactive services. Many analysts are expressing concern that traditional shops are not faring well against the interactive agencies. Some claim that the traditional agencies simply waited too long to move in the interactive direction, while others claim that interactive services are just getting started. While interactive divisions generally find that their clients are handed down from their parent company, the interactive agencies are dominating the marketplace.

The interactive agencies are competing head to head with each other for business, but rarely do they find themselves competing with an internal division.

Box 6.3 ■ IBM E-COMMERCE CAMPAIGN

Ogilvy's award-winning campaign for IBM's e-commerce division employed a media mix that included the Web. It opened the campaign with multipage advertising in the *Wall Street Journal* that included IBM's Web site URL. It followed up with a flight of television commercials, targeted ads in trade publications, direct mail packages, and banner ads—all of which directed people to IBM's Web site where customers received the actual selling message.

The agency won a Gold Clio and several other prestigious advertising awards for its IBM e-commerce campaign. Additionally, its e-commerce banners won silver and gold Interactive Pencil awards for best interactive campaign and best single interactive banner (see http://www.ogilvy.com/o_interactive/who_frameset.asp) (Kindel, 1999; "Winner of the Most," 1999).

Selecting an Interactive Agency

Methods of choosing an interactive shop over a traditional agency division include word-of-mouth, in-house searches, and consultation. Questions arise as to what interactive shops should do, how they should be evaluated, and whether they should be evaluated using typical agency criteria. Interactive agency review is the latest business sweeping the industry. With fees for interactive projects ranging from $500,000 to $5 million and more, many clients gladly hire a consultant who will hook them up with the right agency for their needs. Consulting services also charge interactive agencies for listings with their services, often leaving smaller shops with less money out of the loop. Interactive shop reviews are not yet common but many in the industry have taken to the idea and are willing to let consultants team them with clients.

Box 6.4 ■ SEARCHING FOR AN INTERACTIVE AGENCY—
                REQUEST FOR PROPOSAL

Send to the Agency:

- a description of the project's scope, goals, and objectives and the Internet technology environment.
- specific performance requirements (transaction volume for e-commerce, minimum levels of service).
- instructions so an agency knows how to respond.

Request from the Agency

- a basic introduction and agency overview.
- examples of the agency's work, including portfolio and case studies.
- examples of similar projects, if any.
- proof of ability to creatively integrate technology and business skills.
- demonstration that the agency can partner well with marketing and technology departments or other agencies.
- resumes and references of key agency personnel.

(Snyder & Cuneo, 1998).

Traditional agencies are stepping up their interactive divisions to accommodate the needs of cybermarketers. Contemporary agencies bring Web developers together with advertising experts to plan and design online ads and campaigns that are graphically appealing and yet sophisticated enough to produce brand recognition and sales. Agencies are passing the cyberword on to their clients who are learning how to make the most of this new interactive medium through the creation of catchy online banners and effective Web sites.

Although many agencies have yet to see profits from client Web page design, ad creation, or selling ad space, they anticipate that online advertising will be hugely profitable in the near future. The Web is still so new and uncharted that many agencies struggle with determining appropriate fees for interactive work and for creating online campaigns and banner ads. Agencies must also negotiate the lowest possible price for their clients who buy Web ad space, but at the same time they need to get the highest price possible for their clients who offer ad space for sale on their sites.

Online Ventures Turn to Traditional Advertising Agencies

The boundaries between offline and online advertising blur when online companies hire traditional agencies to handle their online and offline ad campaigns. Autobytel.com Inc. (http://auto-by-tel.com), one of the more popular online car buying services, employs Grey Advertising in New York to handle its advertising efforts. Autobytel originally hired Grey Interactive, a division of Grey Advertising, to manage its online advertising but needed to take its business to the next level. A senior vice president for Autobytel explains the selection of Grey Advertising: "The large traditional marketers built their brands with large traditional agencies. To help us become a household name like P&G, we wanted an agency known for building brands globally with expertise beyond the Internet" (Elliott, 1998).

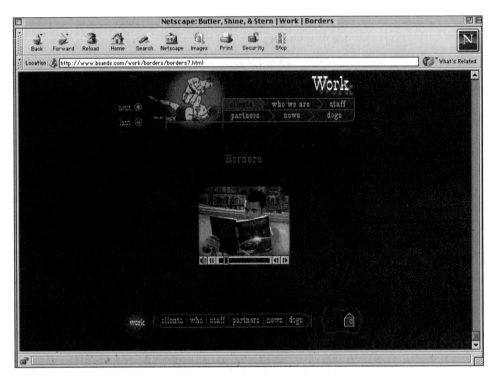

FIGURE 6.1 Borders.com Commercial from Butler, Shine & Stern Site,
http://www.bsands.com/work/borders/borders7.html

The very competitive online book industry is just as competitive in its search
for agencies. BooksOnline (http://booksonline.com) awarded its $30 million
launch to OgilvyOne Worldwide, New York, while TBWA Chiat/Day handles
Barnes & Noble online (http://www.barnesandnoble.com). Foote, Cone & Belding San Francisco created campaigns for Amazon.com, and Borders Books
(http://www.borders.com) has placed its online ads (Figure 6.1) under the care of
Butler, Shine & Stern (http://www.bsands.com) of Sausalito, California (Petrecca
& Snyder, 1998).

Other Alternatives

When Williams-Sonoma, the giant housewares retailer, first started thinking of developing an online presence, it knew it had to hire an agency with e-commerce experience—one that could handle its aggressive marketing plans. Williams-Sonoma
selected USWeb/CKS (http://uswebcks.com), a full-service firm with expertise in
strategic marketing, customer relationship management, resource planning, strategic branding and advertising, systems integration, network design, and e-commerce.
USWeb/CKS also handles the online and traditional media advertising for Levi-Strauss's e-commerce sites. Businesses such as Williams-Sonoma that are integrat-

ing their online and offline components are relying less on traditional advertising agencies and interactive shops and moving toward full-service interactive firms (Johnson, 1998; Williamson, 1999).

Jupiter Communications has identified at least eight categories of Web development/advertising/marketing firms available for hire. When it comes to establishing an online site, several different firms are hired rather than just one agency. For instance, when Nike wanted to start selling products online, it turned to several companies for help: Red Sky Interactive (creative and site production), Digex (Web and applications hosting), Fort Point Partners (systems integration), Cyber-Source (credit card security), and InterWorld Corporation (e-commerce), but Nike's advertising agency, Wieden & Kennedy, had little to do with the project (Williamson, 1999).

SALES FORCE

Many agencies are competing with big-name technology companies (such as Microsoft and Dell Computer) as well as Web development and data warehousing companies for employees with Internet technology experience. Agencies are facing a host of challenges in attracting workers with skills in electronic commerce, programming, up-to-date technology, and advertising/marketing. Traditional and interactive agencies are feeling the pinch as young new media-experienced talent accept offers from high tech companies. Competition is only going to heat up as 1.3 million Internet technology workers will be needed across various industries in the first 3 years of the new century (Gilbert, 1999b).

Many traditional agencies are going out of their way to attract sales personnel with backgrounds in advertising as well as the Web. As added incentive, agencies are offering stock options, high salaries, and excellent working conditions. They are even scouring universities' interactive and new media programs for soon-to-be-graduates. Other companies are offering bonuses to current employees who recommend new hires. Some agencies have found that young defectors now equipped with extensive Internet experience can be lured back from dot.coms (Freeman, 1999a; 1999b).

Many media companies with Web space to sell are assembling special advertising sales teams separate from their traditional sales force. Time Warner has a separate group of representatives who sell ads for its online magazines such as Time.com, Money.com, Entertainment Online, and People Online. Besides selling available ad space, the cyber sales force also assists advertisers with online ad design. Many advertisers do not know how to design effective online ads so they depend on the cyber sales teams to step in and create ads that are engaging, interesting, and eye-catching (Huhn, 1995) (see http://www.pathfinder.com/adinfo/adkit/over.html).

The television network CBS considers the Web a separate medium from its other operations, and, rather than hiring a cyber sales force, it employs an outside firm that specializes in Internet sales. CBS follows the philosophy that sales representatives should have a deep understanding of the Internet because online sales are much different from broadcast sales. CBS hires salespeople with extensive Web backgrounds to sell Web space and saves those with expertise in broadcast sales to sell radio and television time (Williamson, 1996a).

SUMMARY

Agencies are under increasing pressure from their clients to be all-powerful. Agencies are expected to be expert advertising strategists and creative gurus, and they must also be Web site and e-commerce developers, multimedia and Internet technology wizards, database managers, and direct marketers, and they must be ready and able to serve any number of other new media functions.

Many agencies are rising to the occasion by developing interactive divisions and by handling marketing efforts beyond advertising. Other agencies are purchasing stand-alone interactive firms to broaden their capabilities. Outsourcing interactive work is an option that agencies also find attractive so they can concentrate on traditional advertising while leaving the online services to those with that type of expertise.

Advertising agencies that will be successful in the new millennium are those who adapt to the new media environment. Whether it is called multimedia, interactive, direct marketing, Internet marketing/advertising, integration, convergence, or whatever new term that is out there, agencies must move in these new directions to thrive and survive. More importantly, they will need to find what they do best and they will need to be the best at what they do.

Agencies should focus on serving their clients and delivering an audience through whatever medium is most effective. Flexibility will be key as agencies quickly move among electronic, print, and Internet venues. Agency personnel of the twenty-first century will be those with technological expertise and technology experts with advertising/marketing experience.

Internet advertising is a new phenomenon brought on by the commercialization of the Web. Advertisers have found a new way to reach global as well as local customers and they are leaning on their agencies to put their promotional messages online. Agencies must adapt to interactivity. How they adapt and their flexibility will be key to their success.

Discussion Questions

1. What characteristics of small and medium-sized agencies have allowed them to lead the large agencies in online advertising?
2. What are the advantages and disadvantages of agencies developing their own internal interactive departments?
3. What are the advantages and disadvantages of agencies shopping out work to independent interactive firms?
4. What kinds of skills do you think you should acquire if you want to work as an agency's account executive?

Chapter Activities

1. Explore a traditional advertising agency's Web site. Note the agency's background, client list, and corporate structure. Does it have an internal interactive department or does it outsource its work?
2. Create your own advertising agency. What services would your firm provide and how would it handle online campaigns?
3. Write a fictional resume that you believe would get you hired at an advertising agency, especially one that includes an interactive department. Include a statement of goals and objectives, educational background, work experience, and other Internet skills.
4. Explore several ad agency sites and look at their interactive work. Who are their clients? What types of banner ads have they produced? What other interactive work have they created?

References

Aaker, D., Batra, R., & Myers, J. G. (1992). *Advertising management.* Englewood Cliffs, NJ: Prentice Hall.

Bayne, K. M. (1998, June 8). AdKnowledge rolls out Web ad evaluation tool. *Advertising Age* [Online]. Available: http://www.adage.com/interactive/articles/19980608/article3.html (1999, September 17).

Blankenhorn D. (1999, March 1). DoubleClick sharpens customer focus. *Advertising Age, 70* (9), p. s12.

Carmichael, M. (1998, March 9). Brochureware dominates in survey of agency sites. *Advertising Age,* p. S7.

Elliott, S. (1998, November 24). Internet companies turn to traditional ad firms. *The New York Times on the Web* [Online], Available: http://www.nytimes.com (1999, February 19).

Forrester Research, Inc. (1996). *Media & Technology Strategies.* [Online]. Available: http://www.forrester.com (1998, January 21).

Freeman, L. (1999a, October 4). Net slashes time from hello to adios. *Interactive Week, 70* (41), p. 42.

Freeman, L. (1999b, July 26). Some agencies learn to recruit at Internet speed. *Advertising Age, 70* (31), pp. s31, s34, s40.

Gilbert, J. (1999a, March 1). Agencies centralize Web ad serving. *Advertising Age, 70* (9), pp. s1, s18.

Gilbert, J. (1999b, March 15). Agencies pursue hot tech workers. *Advertising Age, 70* (11), pp. 42, 45.

Gilbert, J. (1999c, April 19). MediaCom opens interactive buying division. *Advertising Age, 70* (17), p. 68.

Gilbert, J. (1999d, July 26). Web shops savor their differences from ad agencies. *Advertising Age, 70* (39), pp. s14, s16, s18.

Gleason M., & Williamson, D. A. (1996, February 26). The new interactive agency. *Advertising Age,* p. s1.

History. (1999). *Agency.com Web site* [Online]. Available: http://www.agency.com/our-company/history (2000, February 10).

Huhn, M. (1995, March 20). Time taps WWW sales unit. *MediaWeek, 5* (12) p. 6.

Johnson, B. (1998, August 31). Levi's goes offline to plug Web stores. *Advertising Age, 70* (25), p. 2.

Kindel, S. (1999, Fall). Brand champion. *Critical Mass,* pp. 56–58.

Maddox, K., & Bruner, R. E. (1998, January 26). New services automate online media planning. *Advertising Age,* p. 38.

Napoli, L. (1996). Omnicom boutique investments mark turning point for advertising on the Web. *New York Times—CyberTimes* [Online]. Available: http://search.nytimes.com/Web/docsroot/library/cyber/week/1018omnicom.html

New roll-up player gobbles NY firms, files for IPO. (1999, June 11). *At New York* [Online]. Available: http://atnewyork.com/news1.htm (1999, September 27).

Outing, S. (1997, June 28). Regional Web ad program. *Editor & Publisher* [Online]. Available: http://www.mediainfo.com

Petrecca L., & Snyder, B. (1998, July 27). Ogilvy-One wins role in online book wars. *Advertising Age, 69* (30), pp. 1, 31.

Riedman, P. (1996, January/February). Netscape. *Creativity*, (4), pp. 24–25.

Riedman, P. (1999, July 26). Watching the e-parade. *Advertising Age, 70* (31), pp. s20, s22, s24.

Snyder, B., & Cuneo A. Z. (1998, September 14). Consultants tap market for Web agency searches. *Advertising Age, 69* (37), pp. 46, 53.

Taylor, C. (1996, October 7). Agreeing and disagreeing: CASIE and the Internet Ad Bureau spar over advertising size. *MediaWeek, 6* (38), p. 3.

Tedeschi, B. (1999, June 21). Net companies look offline for consumer data. *The New York Times on the Web* [Online]. Available: http://www.nytimes.com/library/tech/99/06/cyber/commerce/21commerce.html (1999, July 14).

Voight, J. (1996, December). Beyond the banner. *Wired*, p. 196.

Vonder Haar, S. (1999a, October 11). CMGI to launch Web-based ad network. *Interactive Week, 6* (29), p. 22.

Williamson, D. A. (1995, July 17). When buyers become sellers. *Advertising Age, 66*, p. 12.

Williamson, D. A. (1996, January 9). CBS to outsource Web ad sales. *Advertising Age, 67*, p. 3.

Williamson, D. A. (1997, February 24). Online buying moves towards a virtual market. *Advertising Age, 68* (8), p.76.

Williamson, D. A. (1999, July 26). Agencies left in the cold as marketers expand online. *Advertising Age, 70*, (31), pp. s26, s28, s30.

Winner of the most industry awards in 1999. (1999). *Ogilvy Interactive* [Online]. Available: http://www.ogilvy.com/o_interactive/who_frameset.asp

Chapter 7

Banner Design
and Banner Awards

Web advertising is relatively new to the online world and the technology and design of ads on the Web remains a new area of study. Although the standard forms are still developing, generally, Web ads are referred to as banners—rectangular-shaped two-dimensional insertions on Web sites or in text. The goal of a banner is first to attract attention and then to get the audience to pursue more information that will lead to a sale, brand awareness, or some other marketing objective. Since technologically sophisticated, media-rich banners are, at present, very slow loading and therefore undesirable to the audience, the construction and placement of a simple banner is critical for advertising success on the Web.

    This chapter will discuss some of the basics about Web advertising design and construction. In addition, tips to creating an effective banner will be explored. Finally, competitions and awards for excellence in Web advertising will be discussed and readers will be referred to examples of award winning banner advertisements.

DESIGNING ADS FOR THE WEB

Since the first banner ad appeared in 1994, the technology of advertising on the Web has changed considerably. What was first a rectangular banner similar to a display ad in print advertising has been evolving into a space on a Web site that can lead to an intriguing journey to learn more about products and services. Clicking on a banner can send the visitor to a larger version of the ad with more information, both visual and textual. Clicking can also lead to an opportunity for the visitor to interact with the advertiser by asking for more information, requesting a newsletter, downloading in-depth information or user information like recipes, or simply purchasing the product. As the interaction between the visitor and the ad becomes more involved and sophisticated, so do the requirements for designing and creating the banner ad and the links from it. Software for the creation of ads on the Web has become more sophisticated, allowing ad design to be more accessible to advertising practitioners and not just those who have extensive training in computer programming and HTML coding.

Designing Banner Ads

Researchers at Jupiter Communications have conducted studies that seem to indicate that banner ads are dropping in effectiveness. Specifically, click-through rates (CTRs) from banners had fallen to "a quarter of what they were in 1997." This drop occurred despite the predictions that online advertising will gross over $22 billion by the year 2004, accounting for about 8 percent of the entire advertising industry. Obviously, industry visionaries seem to think that banner ads, regardless of evidence to the contrary, will continue to generate many advertising dollars ("Promised Land.com," 1999).

Banner advertising, while similar to billboards or just about any print media embedded display ad, does not have much to offer unless it is at least somewhat compelling. If it does not grab the surfer, it will do nothing. The real goal for banner advertising is to stop a surfer and cause that person to delve into the content that the banner has to offer. Some say that the real breakthrough for banner advertising will be when the technology of **bit streaming** has been brought to the point where banner ads can lead a consumer to a full frame ad with pictures, motion, and sound that compares to what consumers see on television. Clicking on banner advertising is truly voluntary, unlike television, radio, billboards, and print ads that appear before audiences can ignore them. Banner ads offer advertising messages for those who choose to interact with them—the consumer must first choose to investigate what the banner has to offer by clicking through it. Without compelling content, consumers will surf, not dive in.

Internet ads must work hard to attract attention and be effective. While network style video is not going to be technically feasible for some time, banner designers will have to rely on creativity and ingenuity to attract the targeted audience. The ability to innovate will become more important than ever to advertisers as click-through rates drop because banner ads lose the ability to hold attention.

The decrease in click-through rates is due at least in part to a desensitization effect that has occurred since the mid-1990s.

Goals

The state of the art of Web advertising has progressed to the point where practitioners are trying to establish realistic, measurable goals for their work. Obviously, neither hits nor click-through rates are specific enough to give the necessary feedback about advertising success.

Advertisers need to set goals for their banners that correspond with their reasons for advertising online in the first place. If an advertiser desires to increase brand awareness, then the advertising campaign or banners should be designed for this purpose. If an advertiser wants to increase online sales, then perhaps an interactive banner with order capabilities is appropriate. In any case, advertisers need to set clear and obtainable goals to direct the design and placement of their banners and other online ads.

Creating an Effective Banner Ad

With click-through rates falling plus the number of Web sites and clutter at Web sites constantly increasing, advertisers are feeling pressure to create banners that can attract attention and get action. Advertising agencies and their online departments are scrambling to get information about how to make their Web advertising more effective. There are a number of sources for information regarding Web site advertising effectiveness that base their recommendations on both statistically monitoring existing sites for results and personal experience that has yielded the outcomes desired. Variables that have been explored by these sources include market targeting, timing of placement, location at the site, bandwidth or size considerations, interactivity, physical size, colors, font style, and word selection.

Targeting

A basic tenet of advertising is that ads work best when people who are potential customers for the product can see them. It does no good to get high click-through rates and attention from audience members who are not going to be customers despite persuasive advertising. This indicates the need for appropriate media selection in the practice of selecting sites for advertising that attract the market targeted for the product to be advertised. Generally speaking, banners should be placed close to Web pages that have content related to the product or service in the banner, and banners should be designed to attract the desired audience.

Banner Ad Sizes

Standardization is common in the advertising industry as television and radio commercials typically run 15, 30, 45, or 60 seconds long. Most print publications size their advertisements according to a standardized system of column inches.

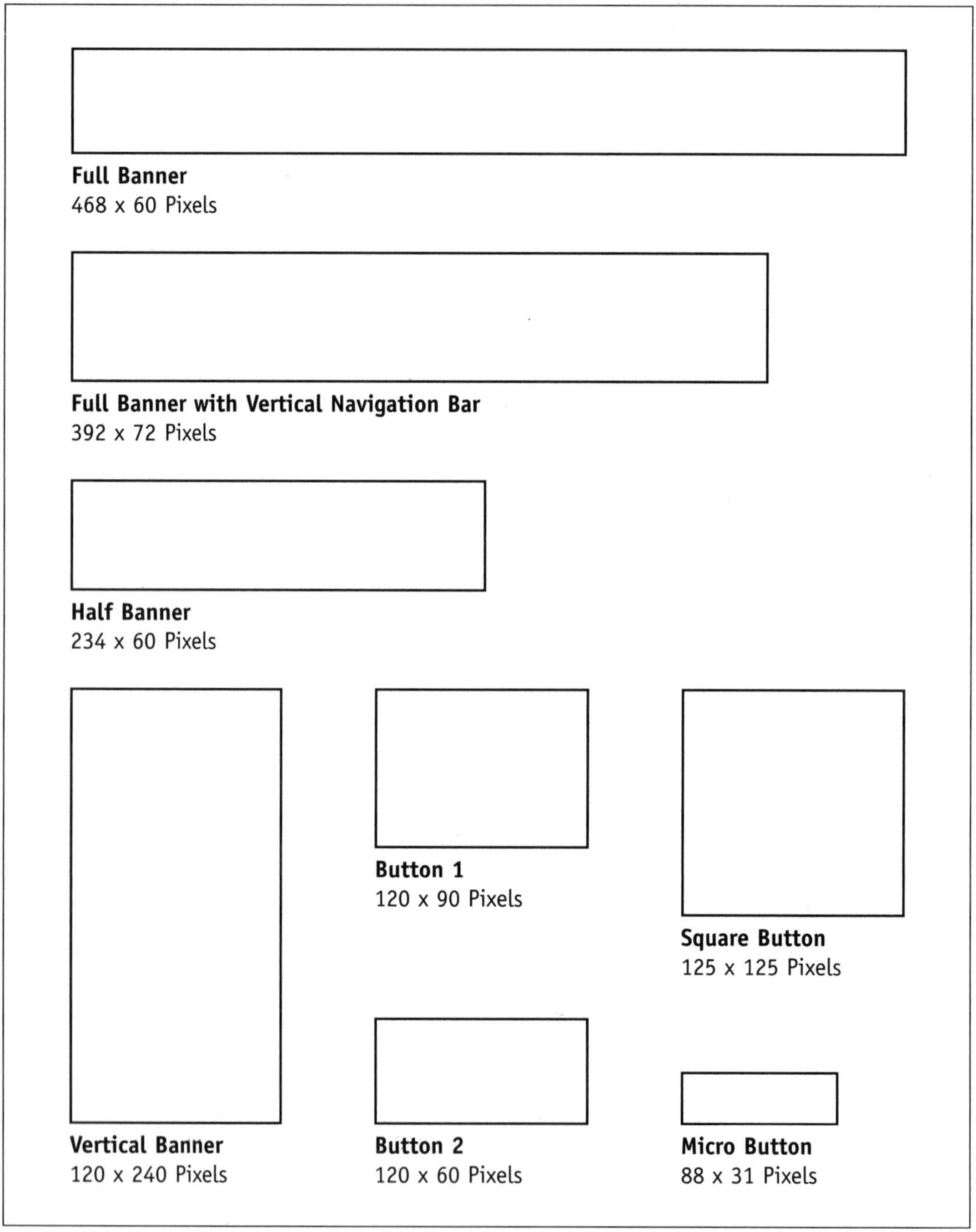

Full Banner
468 x 60 Pixels

Full Banner with Vertical Navigation Bar
392 x 72 Pixels

Half Banner
234 x 60 Pixels

Button 1
120 x 90 Pixels

Square Button
125 x 125 Pixels

Vertical Banner
120 x 240 Pixels

Button 2
120 x 60 Pixels

Micro Button
88 x 31 Pixels

FIGURE 7.1 IAB Ad Sizes, **(http://www.iab.net/iab_banner_standards/
bannersource.html)**

Establishing standard sizes of online ads is a challenging task but one that needs to be undertaken. Without standardization, designers must make significant changes in their Web sites to accommodate various sized banners and advertisers must spend the extra time and money it takes to resize ads to fit each site's specifications (Taylor, 1996).

Few disagree that standardization is necessary, but few agree on the standard sizes. The Internet Advertising Bureau (IAB) (Figure 7.1) proposed eight standard sizes for banner ads, several of which did not coincide with many of the sizes set forth by the Coalition for Advertising Supported Information and Entertainment (CASIE). For instance, the current most common size for banner ads, 468 × 60 pixels, was not among the six standard banner sizes recommended by CASIE, causing the IAB to balk at CASIE's recommendations (Taylor, 1996). More recently, the two organizations jointly recommended the following most common banner sizes (in pixels):

468 × 60 full banner

392 × 72 full banner with vertical navigation bar

234 × 60 half banner

125 × 125 square button

120 × 90 button #1

120 × 60 button #2

88 × 31 micro button

120 × 240 vertical banner

Finding Images

Creating simple banners can be accomplished by using a solid color background and an interesting font for the text. It is best to keep it simple whenever possible for two reasons. First, without a familiarity with HTML code and the possession of art skills, it may be much easier to pay a person who works with creating Web pages and Web advertising on a regular basis. Second, keep in mind that small file sizes can lead to better audience response. Simple backgrounds allow smaller file sizes and, thus, less downloading time.

If it is desirable to add sophisticated images to the banner, it might be best to find a file with the desired image already in it. There are several services that specialize in finding images. These visual search engines can locate images either by entering keywords as in a standard Web search or by sending an image similar to the one being sought. Two companies that perform this service are ditto.com (http://www.ditto.com) and Northern Light (http://www.northernlight.com).

Timing   Advertisers who place their commercials on radio or television have known for a long time that not only must the correct station or network be selected, but also the correct time of day must be selected for success. Standard broadcast media have become predictable in terms of when the largest audience will be watching or listening. In radio, morning drive time (6 to 9 A.M.) and afternoon drive time (3 to 6 P.M.) enjoy the largest audiences of the day. In television, the audience size peaks during local news times (6 and 10 P.M. or 6 and 11 P.M.) and all of prime time. Advertisers are just now learning about peak times on the Web. Cyberbucks do go a bit further at certain times of the day.

Web activity during lunch hour is higher than at morning times. Response at this time can be up to 25 percent higher than at other times, according to a vice president of advertising agency MMG Inc. (http://www.mmgco.com) (Vonder Haar, 1998b). Other good times for Web activity have been found to be between 5 and 6 P.M. and after 10 P.M. Even though advertisers may be aware of the best times to have their banner appear, ads can rarely be bought and placed in this manner.

Placement   New research has shown that banners placed at the bottom right of the screen next to the scroll bar and those placed one-third of the way down from the top generate more clicks than banners placed elsewhere. Web site providers and advertisers can use this information to their advantage.

Web site design managers can design pages with banner spots placed in the most visible and clickable places on the page. Advertisers can design ads that look like an extension of the editorial content and insist that their banners be placed in the best spots on the page. Also, advertisers can promote products that are relevant to editorial content. For more specific information about banner placement, try the Webreference Banner Ad Placement Study site (http://www.webreference. com/dev/banners/research.html).

File Size   There is a natural tendency for people who first design ads for the Web to utilize the "whiz bang" aspects of the Web to get and hold attention for their ads. This may be effective for other media, such as television, where computer-generated commercials complete with interesting shapes, bright colors, lots of movement, likeable characters, and catchy music are likely to get attention from the audience. Commercials for Budweiser beer had animated, lifelike lizards who often told jokes and complained about not getting as much attention as the Budweiser frogs who croaked "Bud," "wei," and "ser." This campaign lasted for more than a year because of its novelty and cleverness.

Newspapers command a premium from advertisers that use color in their ads because color ads stand out in mostly black and white newspapers. All other things being equal, this can be true of advertising on the Web also. It is common knowledge among video practitioners that our eyes are attracted to bright colors and movement (Medoff & Tanquary, 1998). This effect has been seen in banner ads because some banners with animation have shown terrific response rates (Cleland & Carmichael, 1997). A brightly colored banner ad or one with animation should attract more attention than one with dull colors or static presentations. The problem with this comparison on the Web is that all other things are not equal. That is, Web advertisers make a big sacrifice in order to have fancy banner ads. That sacrifice is bandwidth. Banners with animation, complex patterns, audio, video, or interactivity require a much larger file than simpler banner ads.

There is research that encourages advertisers to have slowly loading banners. An animated banner ad facilitates a quicker reaction time and generates better recall than still banner ads. In addition, large banner ads enhance reaction time and trigger more clicks than small banner ads (Li & Bukovac, 1999).

Even though industry executives say that banner ads must be compelling enough to get users away from other site content and that banners that offer interactivity will generate more interest in banners (Vonder Haar, 1998a), some recent studies have shown otherwise. When researchers asked people to seek information placed in a blinking banner ad on a Web page, they found that people sometimes ignored animated ads. In fact, some users even covered the ad with their hands. Other simply refused to look at the blinking ad. Another study found that colorful graphics or "pretty pictures" appealed to only 5 percent of the people surveyed (Hamilton, 1999).

Another study has shown that the length of time it takes for a banner to load is critical. Six banners were constructed that looked identical, but they had slightly different background patterns. The background pattern differences did not seem to be noticeable, so the only real difference among these banners was file size.

Click-through rates for the banners after 5,000 exposures were

1. 2,477 bytes, CTR = 2.60%
2. 5,161 bytes, CTR = 2.32%
3. 6,630 bytes, CTR = 1.35%
4. 7,422 bytes, CTR = 1.29%
5. 9,742 bytes, CTR = 1.18%
6. 10,149 bytes, CTR = 1.12%

Despite the similar appearances in the banners, each had a different loading time because of its file size. The results show that loading time makes a difference. As file size decreases, the CTR increases. For more about this relationship, visit the Bannertips site (http://www.bannertips.com/sizematters.shtml).

Software programs exist that will compress files needed to produce a banner ad. One program that became available recently, GifWizard (http://www.gifwizard.com/pn=43272) can compress graphics up to 90 percent.

Engage Media has come up with a way to give its clients a helping hand when it comes to rich media. It has introduced a new rich-media program, ResponsePoint, that makes it easy for advertisers to create ads with scrolling forms, Java animation, audio, video, transaction capabilities, and other enhanced features. Additionally, sites connected through the Engage Media network can now support the rich-media ads without overly long downloading times (Maddox, 1998a). Despite the difficulties, rich-media ads are gaining in popularity and use as Internet technology improves and bandwidth and transmission speeds increase.

Keywords   One way of making sure that advertising is seen on a Web page is to make sure that many people find the Web page. A technique for accomplishing just that has to do with words that are used in the banner ad itself. Keywords are words that are used by search engines to help people find things on the Web. Sometimes these are single words that stand alone and are self-explanatory. To get a map of a particular area, a user may simply enter the word *map* into a search engine. The engine would then provide a list of sites that have the word *map* in them. With a bit of luck, the appropriate site will be listed and the user can click on that link to be taken to a site that will provide the desired map. Another technique and one that works better would be to include another word or two that would narrow the search to only those sites that have the specific information requested. Savvy Webmasters who want their sites found easily and quickly will make sure that their Meta tag (part of the head of an HTML document that provides information for search robots) and site contain keywords that are very popular. By doing so, they increase the chances that their Web sites will get listed for many of the searches performed by users.

This general technique can also be applied to banner advertising. Banners that contain very popular words may be included in the lists provided by search engines. Box 7.1 lists 10 of the most popular search words entered by search engine users at the Goto.com site (http://www.goto.com) (sex-related words are removed). By using some of these words in their banner ads, advertisers can increase page views considerably.

Box 7.1 ■ TOP 10 SEARCH WORDS, NOVEMBER 1998

1. games	3. travel	5. sports	7. free stuff	9. books
2. music	4. maps	6. jobs	8. yahoo	10. software

In addition to the top 10 words, top search words can also be found and used if relevant. Some companies sell lists of search words to Webmasters who want to make sure that they use keywords that are currently popular. Another site to try for current keywords and key phrase lists is the Mall-net (http://www.mall-net.com/se_report/#use) site. This site offers a variety of lists of words and phrases that are popular. In early 2000, words or terms like *mp3, pokemon, yahoo, hotmail, warez, linux, jokes,* and *games* were popular.

Miscellaneous Tips   Quite a few people who work with banner advertising on the Web are willing to give advice on maximizing banner effectiveness. Here is a condensed version of some of the wisdom available regarding constructing, designing, and placing banner ads.

- Give instructions or directions to the audience. Most commonly, this would be the ubiquitous "Click Here!" Some practitioners like to use urgency . . . the "last-chance" appeal.
- Get the attention of the audience. Many practitioners believe that the use of the word free can be very powerful. Attention can also be gained through a variety of techniques, such as the use of animation, bright colors, and splashy

design. Try to involve the audience—interactivity works. Ask for answers or comments. Stimulate audience curiosity; make them guess at least a little.

■ Keep banners fresh. Change copy and or design regularly.

■ Target the banner. Hit the audience at the right level.

■ Contests do not appear to be very effective. Avoid wasting too much time and money on them.

■ Keep the banners small (in bytes) to allow them to load quickly. Some practitioners believe that large physical size helps a banner produce better.

■ Intrigue and sex sell (at least, up to a point).

■ Tracking banner effectiveness will lead to better banners.

■ Links from the banner should be product specific. Avoid linking the audience to a home page or page with many products or services. Make the link to a page that will get the audience behavior desired by the advertiser.

■ When in doubt, keep it simple. It is easy to get carried away with tricks and frills.

■ The purpose of a banner is not just to impress the audience, but to get results.

■ Keep the process of "conversion" simple. Try to keep the number of clicks needed for a user to sign up or buy at a minimum.

■ Place the company's signature or logo on the banner to help build branding.

For more information about banners and tips on how to produce effective banners, try the Digiware Interactive Multimedia (http://www.bannertips.com/digiwaretips.shtml), Thunderlizard Productions (http://www.thunderlizard.com), Bannertips (http://www.bannertips.com), and eboz (http://www.eboz.com/advice/banner_advertising/) sites.

AWARDS FOR ONLINE ADVERTISING

Even though it is an industry that is relatively young, Internet advertising already generates billions in advertising revenue. The huge revenue indicates that many people are involved in the planning and creation of Internet advertising. Older media have been recognizing excellence in advertising for many years, but excellence in Internet advertising is just now gaining recognition. The remainder of this chapter will discuss how some organizations that have traditionally recognized advertising excellence are now giving awards to professionals who present their work on the Web.

Clio Awards

The Clio Awards have been the world's largest advertising competition, presenting hundreds of awards over the past 40 years to the industry's top examples of advertising. Although best known for honoring creative television ads, these annual awards are also given to advertising's best work in radio, print, outdoor, integrated media, package design, student work, and, recently, Web sites and Web advertising.

For the past few years, Clio awards have been given for the category Best Web Site. In 1999, the advertising executives who make selections for Clios decided to break out advertising on the Web as a separate category. The categories for the first year of Web-related awards were

artistic technique

brand building

consumer targeted sites

direct response

e-commerce

Internet rich-media advertising

relationship marketing

self-promotion

The Clio award is the oldest and arguably the most prestigious award given for excellence in advertising. The decision to award Clios for online advertising has given the Web credibility as a viable and important advertising vehicle. David Badagliacca of DNA Studio was awarded a Clio in the category of artistic technique. Badagliacca said, "This shows that the Web is not just an experiment anymore. It's a real tool now" (Napoli, 1999).

The interactive competition attracted over 400 entries in the first year, with the expectation that the number of entries will grow considerably as the medium itself continues to grow. Many entries came from the big established agencies, but a large number of entries came from smaller agencies that are especially designed to work with the Internet and are better versed in the technology.

Another reason that the Clio organizers decided to give awards for online work is the importance of the medium for advertising and marketing purposes and the strong growth that the medium is experiencing in advertising revenues. Finally, online advertising was given its own Clio awards because of the realization that the Internet can offer advertisers qualities that are not offered by other media. Internet advertising can collect information on customers and prospective customers, while providing the opportunity to offer specific, in-depth product information. Since these aspects of the Internet play a large role in the creation of effective advertising on the Web, treating Internet advertising as if it were the same as advertising in other media is simply a mistake. More information about the Clio Awards and award winners can be found on the Clio Awards site (http://www.clioawards.com).

CASIE Awards

Beginning in 1996, CASIE began giving awards for excellence in interactive advertising (Figure 7.2). Judges for the CASIE awards represent advertising clients, interactive agents, and new media companies. Winners of the CASIE awards tend to have a number of key attributes in common. These attributes include an orientation to consumer needs and interests and an ability to engage the audience with

FIGURE 7.2   1999 CASIE Award Winners, **http://www.casie.com**

a focus on results. Rather than have advertising that is just aesthetically pleasing or entertaining, the winners are those advertisements that emphasize results. In addition to the common measure of page requests and click-throughs, a number of other results of Internet advertising are considered important. These include the number of sales or leads generated from a site, and information such as recipes, product information, or specifications that actually get downloaded from the site. Another result that is considered is how much customer service is provided as a result of consumer visits to the site. Included in the goals for good Internet advertising are considerations such as branding, click-throughs, purchasing, and simple connections to a Web site.

Now that other organizations have begun giving awards for online advertising excellence, CASIE has decided to stop the CASIE awards and focus its efforts on educating online advertisers. CASIE's efforts now include a glossary of Internet advertising terms.

The Tenagra Awards for Internet Marketing Excellence

The Tenagra Awards began in 1994 when the Tenagra Corporation (http://www.tenagra.com) decided to sponsor a competition to recognize achievement for Internet marketing excellence. The awards are given in six categories: Successful

Internet Business Model, Online Public Relations Success, Online Advertising Success, Publication Focused on Internet Marketing, Technical Achievement to Support Internet Marketing, and Individual Contribution to Internet Marketing.

The category Online Advertising Success recognizes significant and innovative achievements and methodologies that have broken new ground in the field of online advertising. This award is not given for any one advertisement; instead, it goes to a company that has demonstrated excellence in its array of advertising work on the Web. For example, in 1999, the award went to Broadcast.com (http://www.broadcast.com), now known as Yahoo! Broadcast for providing unique online advertising opportunities through streaming media programming. Awards were given in 1999 to acknowledge excellence in Internet advertising that was created and shown online during 1998.

THE FUTURE OF ONLINE ADVERTISING RECOGNITION AND AWARDS

Despite online advertising's short history, it already bills more business than outdoor advertising and is expected to bill as much as $4 billion by 2002. As the measurement of the audience improves and Web sites gain in popularity as sites for entertainment and information, advertising billings will grow. Not only will current advertisers spend more, but more types of businesses will advertise online. Until recently, the biggest online advertisers were companies that dealt directly with computers and the Internet—perhaps in part because these companies like the demographics of the audience. But also, these companies believe in the power of the Internet as a medium to reach people differently than traditional advertising vehicles.

As the use of the Internet becomes more pervasive, more mainstream advertisers will begin using the Internet in a comprehensive way. This will lead to more advertising agencies becoming comfortable with using the Internet and more adept at creating interesting and effective online advertising. Other groups will begin to bestow awards for excellence in online advertising. The Advertising Club of New York (http://www.andyawards.com) currently bestows its ANDY awards for advertising excellence in the categories of television, printed materials, newspaper, magazine, and out of home, but does not currently have a separate category for online creativity. This group, as well as others like it across the country, will begin to recognize online work when it becomes commonplace in local advertising agencies.

There are organizations that recognize Web site excellence and may soon extend their categories for competition to advertising on Web sites as well. One such group is the International Academy of Digital Arts and Sciences (http://www.iadas.com/index.phtml). In 2000, this group gave awards for excellence in Web site design in 27 categories ranging from art to weird. Although e-commerce is a category (a recent winner was Amazon.com), advertising was excluded as a category. Perhaps as advertising on Web sites becomes more of a necessity to Web site creators and rich-media ads demonstrate how creative and compelling Web advertising can be, such groups will start handing out advertising awards.

SUMMARY

Web advertising was born in 1994, but it has generated billions in advertising revenue. Both the technology and the techniques for Web advertising are relatively new and changing rapidly. The vast majority of advertising on the Web is in the form of a banner, usually some type of rectangular shape wider than it is high. Clicking on a banner may take the user to another site, often the site of the advertiser. Banners have changed since their inception and offer not only color, text, and simple graphics, but also animation, audio, and even video. Although there was quite a bit of curiosity in 1994 about the banners that were Web advertising, Web users now tend to ignore banner ads.

When designing a banner ad, it is best to have some realistic goals in mind that are not only creative and qualitative (such a building brand loyalty) but also measurable (such as impressions, click-throughs, file sizes, and sales). Realistic goals vary widely according to a number of factors, such as the price of the product and service or the size of the potential market.

Effective banners are created by considering a number of factors such as market target, location at the site, file size, level of interactivity, and physical size. Other factors include colors, font style and keyword selection. Miscellaneous tips for guiding the creation of effective banner ads include suggestions such as give clear directions to the audience (Click Here!), change copy regularly, keep the file size small, stimulate audience interest, and track banner effectiveness.

Even though the practice of Web advertising is relatively new, national awards are being given out for excellence in the field. The most prestigious award given in non-online advertising is the Clio award, which now includes awards for Web advertising in eight categories. The CASIE awards are given in four categories. The Tenagra Corporation's Tenagra Awards for Internet Marketing Excellence include one for Online Advertising Success. As Web advertising becomes more pervasive, the number of awards for excellence is expected to grow.

Discussion Questions

1. How should banners be designed so that they will generate a high response rate?
2. How has giving awards for the best online advertisements boosted the Web's credibility as an advertising medium?
3. What other types of online advertising awards should be granted?
4. At what point does a banner ad become too distracting and thus turn off viewers?

Chapter Activities

1. Design a banner ad including its size, colors, and font. Describe interactive elements and its targeted audience.

2. Conduct an online advertising awards show. Gather at least five ads from various categories (e.g., computers, automotive, sports), and determine which of the ads are the most attractive, which would draw the most users, and which are the most persuasive.

3. Design a plain banner, an interstitial, and a superstitial ad for the same product or service.

References

Cleland K., & Carmichael, M. (1997, January 13). Banners that move make a big impression. *Advertising Age.* Available: http://adage.com/interactive/articles/199/0113/articles.html

Hamilton, A. (1999, August 19). Secrets of super-high Web ad click-through. *ZDNet* [Online]. Available: http://www.zdnet.com/anchordesk/story/story_2439.html

Internet Advertising Report. (1999). *Internet.com internet advertising report* [Online]. Available: http://www.internetnews.com/IAR/

Li, H., & Bukovac, J. (1999). Cognitive impact of banner ad characteristics: An experimental study. *Journalism and Mass Communication Quarterly, 76* (2), pp. 341–353.

Medoff, N., & Tanquary, T. (1998). *Portable Video: ENG and EFP.* Boston: Focal Press, p. 121.

Napoli, L. (1999, June 22). Major advertising awards given for interactive media. *Cybertimes* [Online]. Available: http://search.nytimes.com/search/daily/

Online ad business has a ways to go. (1996, October 6). *Internet Advertising Report* [Online]. Available: http://www.internet.com

Promised Land.com. (1999, August 23). *Adweek,* p. 14.

Taylor, C. (1996, October 7). Agreeing and disagreeing: CASIE and the Internet Ad Bureau spar over advertising size. *Media Week, 6* (38), p. 3.

Vonder Haar, S. (1998a, July 27). Web ads can be a matter of timing. *ZDNet Interactive Week* [Online]. Available: http://www.zdnet.com/intweek/print/980727/340977.html

Vonder Haar, S. (1998b, November 23). Click-through rates in a slide. *ZDNet Interactive Week* [Online]. Available: http://www.zdnet.com/intweek/stories/news/

Appendix

Web Site URLs

URLs are organized by the chapters in which they appear.

Chapter 1 Introduction to the World Wide Web
and Online Advertising

America Online: http://www.aol.com

CNET.com: http://www.cnet.com

HotWired: http://hotwired.lycos.com

Prodigy: http://www.prodigy.com

Webopedia: http://webopedia.internet.com

ZdNet: http://www.zdnet.com

Chapter 2 The Internet Economy

Amazon.com: http://www.amazon.com

Ask Jeeves: http://www.askjeeves.com

Beyond.com: http://www.beyond.com

CDNow: http://www.cdnow.com

CNET: http://www.cnet.com

CNN Interactive: http://www.cnn.com

CoolSavings: http://www.coolsavings.com

Deja.com: http://deja.com

Dell Computer: http://www.dell.com

E*Trade: http://www.etrade.com

GoTo.com: http://goto.com

Internet Advertising Bureau: http://www.iab.net

Hallmark: http://www.hallmark.com

Microsoft Network: http://home.microsoft.com

RealBet: http://www.realbet.com

Swiffer: http://www.swiffer.com

USA Today: http://www.usatoday.com

USA Today Marketplace: http://www.usatoday.com/marketpl/
mkthome.htm

USA Today Sponsor Index: http://www.usatoday.com/ads.htm

Wedding Channel: http://www.weddingchannel.com

Worth Global Style Network: http://www.wgsn.com/

Yahoo!: http://www.yahoo.com

Chapter 3 Online Ads: What They Are and How They Are Priced

AAddzz: http://www.aaddzz.com

AdCast: http://www.adcast.com

AdKnowledge: http://www.focalink.com/index.html

AdOutlet: http://www.adoutlet.com

Amazon.com: http://www.amazon.com

bcentral: http://www.bcentral.com

Barnes & Noble: http://www.barnesandnoble.com

CarPoint: http://carpoint.msn.com

Cartoon Network: http://www.cartoonnetwork.com

CNN Interactive: http://www.cnn.com

Coolsavings: http://www.coolsavings.com

GoTo.com: http://www.goto.com

H.O.T! Coupons: http://hotcoupons.com

Kids.com: http://KidsCom.com

MSN LinkExchange/bcentral: http://www.adnetwork.bcentral.com

MSN Sidewalk: http://national.sidewalk.msn.com

MSNBC: http://www.msnbc.com

Narrative Communication: http://www.narrative.com

NetRatings: http://www.nielsen-netratings.com

Netscape Communication Corporation: http://www.netscape.com

The New York Times on the Web: http://www.nytimes.com

The New York Times on the Web Online Media Kit: http://www.nytimes.
com/adinfo/rates.html

Nick-at-Nite: http://www.nick-at-nite.com

OneMediaPlace: http://www.onemediaplace.com

Pokemon World: http://www.pokemon.com

RealNet: http://www.realnetworks.com/company/advertising/samples/samples/video.html

Sesame Street: http://www.sesamestreet.com/

SmarkClicks: http://www.smartage.com/smartclicks/index.html

Standard Rate and Data Service (SRDS):   http://www.srds.com/media_resource/index.html

Suck.com: http://www.suck.com

TV Guide Online: http://www.tvguide.com/tv/

USA Today: http://usatoday.com

Value Click: http://valueclick.com/ad.html

Web Digest for Marketers: http://www.wdfm.com/

WDFM's CPM calculator http://www.wdfm.com/advertising/

Wickedslant.com: http://www.geocities.com/SoHo/Lofts/3156/webstrands.html

You Don't Know Jack: http://www.won.net/channels/bezerk/

ZDNet: http://www.zdnet.com

Chapter 4   Online Advertising Opportunities

24/7 Media: http://www.247media.com

Alta Vista: http://www.altavista.com

America Online: http://www.aol.com

Asian Avenue: http://www.AsianAvenue.com

Association of Coupon Professionals: http://www.couponpros.com

Black Voices: http://blackvoices.com

CareerPath: http://careerpath.com

Chicago Tribune: http://chicagotribune.com

Chinese Cyber City: http://ccchome.com

CitySearch: http://www.citysearch.com

Classified Ventures: http://www.classifiedventures.com

CNN Interactive: http://www.cnn.com

Coalition against Unsolicited Commercial E-mail (CAUCE):   http://www.cauce.org

CollegeClub.com.:   http://www.collegeclub.com

Coupon Café: http://www.couponcafe.net

CouponPages: http://www.couponpages.com

The Economist: http://www.economist.com

Environmental News Network: http://www.enn.com

Epicurious: http://www.epicurious.com

eSmarts: http://www.esmarts.com/coupons.html

E-target.com: http://www.e-target.com

Excite: http://www.excite.com

Hotmail: http://www.hotmail.msn.com

H.O.T! Coupons: http://www.hotcoupons.com

Infoseek: http://infoseek.go.com

Jeopardy: http://www.spe.sony.com/tv/shows/jeopardy

Juno Online: http://www.juno.com

LatinoLink: http://www.latinolink.com

Lycos: http://www.lycos.com

Mayo Health Clinic: http://www.mayohealth.org/index.htm

Mind Arrow: http://www.mindarrow.com

Mother Jones: http://www.motherjones.com

MSN: http://www.msn.com

MSN Sidewalk: http://national.sidewalk.msn.com

NetCreations: http://www.netcreations.com

Netscape Communication Corporation: http://www.netscape.com

New Jersey Online: http://www.nj.com

New York Regional Advertising Program (NYRAP):   http://www.
nyrap.com

PlanetOut: http://www.planetout.com

Poweradz: http://www.poweradz.com

Riddler: http://www.riddler.com

SineNet: http://home.sina.com/index.html

Snap: http://www.snap.com

Sony Online Entertainment: http://www.spe.sony.com

Spam.abuse.net: http://spam.abuse.net/

Spam Recycling Center: http://www.chooseyourmail.com/spamindex.cfm

Student Advantage Network: http://www.studentadvantage.com

Talk City: http://www.talkcity.com/chatpages/enter.htmpl

TipWorld: http://www.topica.com/tipworld

Topica: http://www.topica.com

Uproar: http://www.uproar.com

USA.net: http://usa.net

Val-Pak Direct Marketing Systems: http://www.valpak.com

Warner Bros. Online: http://www.warnerbros.com

Wheel of Fortune: http://www.spe.sony.com/tv/shows/wheel

Yahoo!:   http://www.yahoo.com

You Don't Know Jack: http://www.won.net/channels/bezerk

Chapter 5   Web Ratings and Measurement

AdKnowledge: http://www.adknowledge.com

CASIE: http://www.casie.com

Channelseek: http://www.channelseek.com

DoubleClick: http://www.doubleclick.com

Engage Media: http://www.engage.com/engagemedia

GoTo.com: http://www.GoTo.com

HitBox: http://www.hitbox.com

Internet Advertising Bureau: http://www.iab.net

Internet Direct Marketing Bureau: http://www.idmb.org/mission.asp

Matchlogic: http://www.matchlogic.com

Media Metrix, Inc: http://www.mediametrix.com

NetLine: http://www.ipro.com

Nielsen/NetRatings: http://nielsen-netratings.com/hot_off.htm

Peacefire: http://www.peacefire.org

Solid Oak Software: http://www.solidoak.com

WebSideStory: http://www.websidestory.com

Chapter 6   Agency Presence Online

AdKnowledge: http://www.focalink.com/aksystem/index.html

Agency.com: http://www.agency.com

Amazon.com: http://www.amazon.com

Autobytel.com Inc.:   http://auto-by-tel.com

Barnes & Noble: http://www.barnesandnoble.com

BBDO: http://www.bbdo.com

BooksOnline: http://booksonline.com

Borders Books: http://www.borders.com

Butler, Stern & Shine: http://www.bsands.com

CASIE: http://www.casie.com

DDB Needham: http://www.ddbn.com

DoubleClick   http://www.doubleclick.net

Grey Advertising: http://www.grey.com/index3.htm

Infoseek: http://www.infoseek.com

Leo Burnett: http://www.leoburnett.com

Luminant Worldwide Corporation: http://www.luminant.com

Mad Dogs & Englishmen: http://www.maddogadv.com/

McCann Erickson: http://www.mccann.com

Ogilvy & Mather: http://www.ogilvy.com

OmnicomGroup: http://www.omnicomgroup.com

Starcom: http://www.starcommedia.com

TBWA/Chiat/Day: http://www.tbwachiat.com

Time-Warner Pathfinder (Advertising Information): http://www.pathfinder.com/adinfo/adkit/over.html

USWeb/CKS: http://uswebcks.com

Young & Rubicam: http://www.yr.com

Young & Rubicam SF: http://www.yrsf.com/home.html

Chapter 7   Banner Design and Banner Awards

Advertising Club of New York: http://www.andyawards.com

Bannertips: http://www.bannertips.com

Bannertips (design and size): http://www.bannertips.com/sizematters.shtml

Broadcast.com/Yahoo! Broadcast: http://www.broadcast.com

Clio Awards: http://www.clioawards.com

Digiware Interactive Multimedia: http://www.bannertips.com/digiwaretips.shtml

Ditto.com: http://www.ditto.com

eboz: http://www.eboz.com/advice/banner_advertising/

GifWizard: http://www.gifwizard.com/pn=43272

Goto.com: http://www.goto.com

International Academy of Digital Arts and Sciences: http://www.iadas.com/index.phtml

Internet Advertising Bureau: http://www.iab.net/iab_banner_standards/bannersource.html

Mall-net: http://www.mall-net.com/se_report/#use

MMG Inc.: http://www.mmgco.com

Northern Light: http://www.northernlight.com

The Tenagra Corporation: http://www.tenagra.com

Thunderlizard Productions: http://www.thunderlizard.com

Webreference Banner Ad Placement Study: http://www.webreference.com/dev/banners/research.html

Glossary

Terms and (Chapter Number)

Ad auction (3) Online venue where leftover space is bought and sold, often at discounted prices.

Advertiser (2) Private or public company or organization that purchases time or space in the mass media to accomplish a marketing or corporate objective.

Advertising (2) Promotional messages paid for by an identified sponsor for the purpose of influencing an audience.

Advertising exchange (3) Online outlet where Web site providers exchange space on their site for free advertising on another's site.

Advertorial (3) Online promotional message made to look like information.

Andreessen, Marc (1) Headed the development of Mosaic.

ARPAnet (Advanced Research Projects Agency) (1) U.S. agency created to advance computer interconnections that led to the further development of the Internet.

Bandwidth (1) The amount of data that can be electronically transmitted all at once through a communication path, such as a telephone line.

Banner ad (2) Earliest and most prevalent form of online advertising. Banners are typically about 6½ inches wide by about 1 inch high (468 × 60 pixels).

Berners-Lee, Tim (1) "Father of the World Wide Web."

Bit streaming (7) A method of transmitting audio or video matter which allows the information to be played just after it is received without waiting for it to be downloaded or stored.

Blind buy (3) Discounted space sold to advertisers that often know very little about the site, but that are willing to take a risk for prices that are sometimes as low as 20 percent off the full rate.

Cache (3, 5) Storing information for future use.

Cerf, Vinton (1) "Father of the Internet." Early pioneer of the Internet and developer of Internet protocols.

Chat forum (1) Online discussion group that exchanges live, real-time messages.

Click-through (3, 5) When a surfer registers interest in a product or service by clicking on the banner.

Click-through rate (1, 3, 5) A pricing structure for banner ads based on the number of visitors who click-through from an ad to the advertiser's home page.

Cookies (1, 2, 5) Tracks Web travels and saves online visitor information—usually without their knowledge or permission—to create personal files that companies use to customize their Web pages to target individuals.

Cooperative advertising (3) When a Web site gets a percentage of an item sold from its site in exchange for discounting ad space.

Cost-per-thousand (CPM) (3) A pricing structure used to sell print and broadcast media. An effective means of comparing the costs of different media. Calculated by dividing the cost of an advertisement by the number of individuals or households (in thousands) that are reached.

Cost-per-transaction (CPT) (3) An online advertising pricing framework where advertisers are assessed a minimal charge or, in some cases, no charge at all for ad placement. Actual costs are based on some sort of sales criteria, such as the number of products sold as a direct result of the online advertising.

Coupon (4) Product and service discount appearing on the Web that is customized by ZIP codes and printed out for in-store redemption.

Cumulative audience (5) The number of unduplicated homes or persons who are exposed at least once to a given advertisement.

Dot.com (6) Commonly used term to describe online business. The term comes from the popular URL extender *.com*.

Downloading (1) The process by which online images appear on a user's computer screen.

Electronic commerce (e-commerce) (2) Business transactions, such as online purchasing, that are conducted on the Internet.

Electronic mail (1) Also known as *e-mail*. An Internet tool for electronically transmitting messages or documents.

Electronic mailing list (1) Internet mail box/discussion forum for subscribed users managed by LISTSERV and Majordomo among other list servers.

Extramercial (3) Electronic ad placed within a three-inch space to the right of the screen. Usually not visible unless users scroll sideways or their monitor resolution is sized at 832×624 or smaller.

E-mail newsletter (4) Newsletter that is distributed electronically to interested parties.

Fragmentation (2) The multiplicity of Internet sites and documents that are often unrelated and unlinked to each other, creating separate fragments of the Web instead of a single entity.

Graphic interchange format (GIF) (3) Graphic image file.

Hits (3, 5) The number of times a Web site is accessed.

HTML (Hypertext Markup Language) (2,3) Computer language used for Web pages.

Hybrid pricing (3) Online ad pricing structure that combines two cost models such as CPM and click-throughs.

Infomercial (3) Online promotional message made to look like information. Often in the form of a Web site or page within a site.

Interactive agency (6) Advertising agency or creative boutique that specializes in online ad creation.

Interactive departments (agency) (6) Traditional ad agency's separate division or operating unit that develops advertisements and campaigns specifically for the Internet and other multimedia outlets such as CD-ROM.

Interactivity (6) Interactions between parties where both are sources and receivers of information via some sort of communication medium such as a telephone or the Internet.

Interlacing (3) Technology that focuses all the elements of a Web page at the same time by first displaying a low-resolution version of the entire image or page, then the resolution increases in stages until the highest possible resolution is reached and the image or page is fully focused.

Internet (1) A global system of networked computers that share information. It is comprised of as many as 45,000 interconnected subnetworks worldwide with no single owner.

Internet Explorer (1) Web browser developed by the Microsoft Corporation.

Internet service provider (ISP) (5) Company that provides Internet connections to its customers.

Interstitial (1,3)   Ad that appears in a separate browser window for several seconds until a site is fully downloaded.

Intranet (4)   A network using Internet software that transmits proprietary and open information among computers housed within an entity such as a corporation. Intranets are mainly used to share company information and computing resources among employees.

Java (1,3)   A computer language based on FORTRAN C++ that allows animated GIFs and other movement on Web pages.

JavaScripting (4)   A fairly easy to use scripting language used for animating GIFs and other elements of a Web page.

Kilobyte (3)   A measure of information commonly referred to as one thousand bytes (2 to the tenth power bytes or 1,024 bytes).

Marketing (2)   The process of planning and executing the conception, pricing, promotion, and distribution of ideas, goods, and services to create exchanges that satisfy individual and organizational objectives.

Minimum bid price (3)   When online advertisers negotiate for lower rates for electronic ads.

Mosaic (1)   The first Web browser. It simplified Web retrieval through hyperlinks.

Netiquette (4)   Etiquette on the Net. Internet manners.

Netscape Navigator (1)   Web browser developed by Netscape Communications Corporation.

Newsgroup (1)   Electronic bulletin board that acts as a discussion and information exchange forum about a specific topic.

Online advertising (1)   Paid promotional messages, including banners, that appear throughout the Internet in places other than the advertiser's Web sites.

Online advertising revenue (2)   The amount of money that was brought in by selling online ad space.

Online advertising spending (2)   The amount of money that advertisers pay to place their promotions in cyberspace.

Opt-in e-mail (4)   Sending ads via e-mail and electronic newsletters with the recipient's permission.

Opt-in rich-media banner (3)   Standard banner that gives consumers the option of selecting the rich-media version.

Outsourcing (6)   When a traditional advertising agency contracts with another agency, such as an interactive shop, to assist with certain aspects of campaign development or ad design.

Pixels (2)   Short for *picture elements*. Tiny dots of color that form the images on a Web page. Computer monitors display 72 pixels per inch, so one inch equals 72 pixels or dots per inch (dpi).

Pop-up (3)   Interstitial or superstitial that pops up within a new browser window that almost completely covers the screen and requires users to close the window before resuming Web surfing.

Portal (2,4)   Multipurpose mega-site that combines news, entertainment, information, searching, e-mail, chat, one-stop shopping, and other services, all in one location.

Product placement (4)   Advertisers pay to have their product woven into the story lines of movies, television shows, and Web programs such as online soaps.

Regional ad placement service (4)   Online space broker that specializes in buying space on sites that serve local or regional areas.

Rich-media ad (3)   Ad that is animated, contains audio or video, or just flashes, blinks, or makes weird sounds. Rich-media ads typically consume more kilobyte space than traditional text or nonanimated banners.

Robot (5)   A software program that automatically finds, identifies, and indexes information for online databases.

Size-based pricing (3)   An online advertising pricing structure where costs are calculated based on the size of the ad—a fixed dollar amount per pixel.

Sniffer (5)   See *robot*.

Spam (1,4)   Unwanted (junk) promotional e-mail.

Spider (5) see *robot.*

Sponsorship (3, 4) Rather than buying banner ads, many advertisers pay to sponsor Web pages that are closely related to their goods so they can add more content about their product than will fit on a banner ad.

Station log (5) A record kept by radio and television stations of the times programs and commercials were aired.

Sticky product (4) Online game or other interactive component designed to keep users on a site for a long period of time.

Superstitial (3) Rich-media ad that appears in a separate browser window for several seconds until a site is fully downloaded.

Sweepstakes (4) Online strategy to get users to take some action, such as clicking on an ad, in return for a chance to win a prize.

Tearsheet (5) Copy of an ad that runs in print publications. Used to verify that the ad was placed as contracted.

Technical programmer (6) Internet expert who develops and implements the necessary technology needed for online interactivity such as electronic commerce.

Time spent listening (TSL)/time spent viewing (TSV) (3) Audience measurement technique used to calculate the amount of time the audience spends listening to radio and watching television.

Unduplicated audience (5) The number of different people who see or hear an advertisement or a commercial.

Video banner ad (v-banner) (3) Banner ad that contains a short video clip.

Web designer (6) Person with expertise in Web site design, including project management, copywriting, and design.

Web properties (5) The various Web sites owned by a company.

Webmercial (3) New wave of online advertising. Almost television-quality video promotion lasting from about 5 to 30 seconds.

World Wide Web (1) An Internet resource that presents information in text, graphic, video, and audio formats.

DATE DUE